LEST WE FORGET

A WWII 101st Airborne Paratrooper

Francis Russell Snell

On The Cover: This mid 1990s picture of Francis Russell Snell was published in the Static Line, a paratrooper magazine. Taken at the March Air Force Base Air Museum, Riverside, California, it captures a moment of nostalgia as Russ looks back at a vintage C-47. Lest we forget his experiences, the inset photographs show him, 1942, and more recently, September 27, 2005.

LEST WE FORGET

A WWII 101ˢᵗ Airborne Paratrooper

Francis Russell Snell

As told to wife, Marjorie Anne Snell

Copyright © 2016 Marjorie Anne Snell

All rights reserved. No part of this publication may be used or reproduced or transmitted in any form or by any means, electronic or mechanical, including photocopying, recording, or any information storage or retrieval system, without prior written permission from the publisher. Printed in the United States of America.

For permissions and rights, contact:
    Marjorie Anne Snell
    69555 Morningside Drive
    Desert Hot Springs, CA 92241

All imagery courtesy of the author as indicated

Photographs from Family Albums unless otherwise identified

ISBN: 978-1-365-17574-9

First published 2016

Graphic Cover Design Digitizing by Lisa Jo (Snell) Hindsley
Scanning, Digitizing, Format and Publisher Coordination by James Bishop

IN MEMORY OF VETERANS WHO GAVE THEIR LIVES, WITH GRATITUDE FOR THOSE WHO STILL SERVE, AND HOPE THAT FREEDOM FOR OUR FAMILY, FUTURE GENERATIONS, AND ALL FREEDOM-LOVING PEOPLE WILL CONTINUE.

Contents

Introduction

I. Leading up to Another War

II. America Enters Another War

III. Rendezvous With Destiny, 1941

IV. From Furlough to Farewells

V. Screaming Eagle Battles and Challenges

VI. "Home Alive in '45"

VII. Living Legacy of A Greatest Generation Paratrooper

Epilogue

About the Author

Acknowledgments and Credits

Chapter Chronology

Introduction

I. LEADING UP TO ANOTHER WAR

1. A Difficult Childhood Becomes His Strength
   -Russ's Narrative Begins
2. Before the War, 1940
   -The Summer Marjorie Was Born

II. AMERICA ENTERS WWII, 1941

3. How America Responded to Pearl Harbor
   -Russ and Family Hear of Attack
4. Experiencing Pearl Harbor
   -Marjorie's Parents Hear About the Attack
5. Traveling the Train as the War Begins
   -Marjorie's Visit to California

III. RENDEZVOUS WITH DESTINY, 1942

6. Traveling the Trains to Camp Toombs
   -Russ's 101st Airborne Enlistment
7. The Rigors of Paratrooper Training
   -Russ's Band of Brothers Earn Their Wings

IV. FROM FURLOUGH AND FAREWELLS TO FREEDOM

8. Furlough Home With the Family
   -Russ Goes Back Home Again to Indiana
9. Boarding the SS Samaria
   -Russ Becomes Homesick and Seasick
10. From Liverpool to Littlecote
    -Russ in the Estate Barn
11. The Famous Formidable Four
    -Russ Stands Beside Eisenhower, Churchill, Bradley, and Montgomery
12. The Beginning of the End of WWII
    -Russ, The C-47, The Uniforms
13. Crossing the English Channel
    -Russ is Anxious to Jump

V. SCREAMING EAGLE BATTLES AND CHALLENGES

14. Normandy, D-Day, June 6, 1944
    -Russ's Destiny
15. Normandy Nurse
    -Marjorie Imagines Being a WWII Nurse
16. A Purple Heart Recovery
    -Russ is "Fine and Dandy"
17. Zon, Holland, The Market Garden Sunday Punch, September 17, 1944
    -Russ's Oak Leaf Cluster
18. The Military Cadet Nursing Corps
    -If Marjorie Was a WWII Nurse
19. Bastogne, Battle of the Bulge, December 19, 1944
    -Russ's Value for Life, Fear of Death
20. From Landsberg Liberators to the Eagles Nest
    -Russ Injured, Unable to Proceed

VI. "HOME ALIVE IN '45"

21. A President's Death. A Paratrooper's Marriage
    -Russ Transferred to Tennessee Hospital
22. Rations, Crashes, and Blackouts
    -Marjorie's Fears

VII. LIVING LEGACY OF A GREATEST GENERATION PARATROOPER

23. From Languish and Loss to Love Again
    -Russ Was Down, But Never Out
24. Faith, Family, and Future Generations
    -Russ and Marjorie's Retirement

INTRODUCTION
To a WWII 101st Airborne Paratrooper's Story

The historians who evaluate war want to glamorize, intellectualize, romanticize, commercialize, or politicize it, to act as though it had clarity of purpose. The "truth" of the matter is, there is no perfect rational reason to why men act like they do, forcing the effect of war on innocent people. Battle cannot be performed like a musical concert with rhythm, organization, and harmony by an all knowing Conductor General who knows everyone's part to play in the overture of the offensive war.

News Reporters: Can we always trust their honesty, their commitment to report the truth and nothing but the truth? So help them, forgive them God! Who decides what "political correctness" is and when it is appropriate? Brainwashed, biased, learned behaviors, propaganda and beliefs from our background: Right Brain, Left Brain, Right Wing, Left Wing! Every side, every war, every person, we are all influenced.

What have we overlooked, denied, or assumed? What are the facts I never knew? What was I influenced by, imagining and hoping to be true despite my better judgment? Why did we sacrifice the lives of our best young men for a war across the Atlantic during WWII? Much of the results and purpose of that war have now been forgotten. Rather than learning from our past,

Lest We Forget

sometimes it is easier to avoid the emotional stories of our ancestors who sacrificed so much for each of us today and future generations. Lest we forget what wars are fought for, I wonder if we learned from the history of WWII or will history repeat itself? What kind of a war will it be the next time?

Someone else's truth may not be the same as "source" or "proof." When a person is compelled to write, inspired to tell a story that is based on their own personal evidence, emotional involvement, and experiences, it becomes the authors belief that the story must be told for the readers benefit as well. My need to write about my own American hero came from a dream one night that was so full of detail it awakened me with a full memory, forcing me to write down an outline for this narrative biography.

Some things are probably not true, if they are too good to be true. If they are too bad to be true, we want to believe they aren't true either, but the atrocities of the holocaust did happen. I have talked to those who liberated a Concentration Camp and heard their firsthand description of the horrifying smell of burning human flesh in mass burials. I have seen for myself an elderly, stooped-over, silver-haired Polish Jewish man who had a scorched, branded like cattle, serial number burned into his skin. The Nazi Germans, had him labeled as an inferior race. I am married to Francis Russell Snell, a 101st, 506, Company C Paratrooper and

INTRODUCTION

Purple Heart survivor who told me his own firsthand account story he had never told before.

OUR STORY

...is based on the reality of a war history as experienced by "Russ" while a paratrooper, and myself as a little two-year-old Texas Cowgirl. It is also a brief "What if" story, assuming that I was a twenty-year-old nurse at that time, dressing the wounds of the injured during WWII with the imaginary romance storybook of "Falling in Love" 45 years before we actually did! Our script looks back from the current old age of physical restrictions to the energetic years, enjoying our youth as though we were both the same age during the war. It's also looking at and remembering the war realities as we actually experienced them. War happens. It always has. It always will. It happens to everyone in one way or another, no matter what our age, to someone we know, are related to, or were told about. We have all suffered the effect of war to some degree.

Russ and I have an unlikely love story. He says he robbed the cradle, but I say, no I didn't marry a father-figure. I had a good father. Our timing was just right! Once life has been

Lest We Forget

experienced, if one is fortunate enough to develop some maturity, values come together and the difference in years doesn't matter anymore. We are soul mates in spite of our 17 years age difference. He cherishes me and I idolize him. We bring out the best in one another, encourage each others passions, and our love for God, family, and country. His passion since retiring is to swim and play golf, mine is to be an artist, scrapbook our family photographs, and write. Everyone who survives their childhood, has enough to write a book!

We love life. Being with each other is a fulfilling togetherness. Our story is not meant to be charming, clever, or witty. It's not a mystery, or just my dream, but you'll find yourself laughing and crying over our adventurous lives. Our friendship grew before our love did, which we like to think of as the better way, rather than the infatuation of "falling in love."

I
LEADING UP TO ANOTHER WAR

"The destiny of mankind is not decided by material computation when great causes are on the move in the world...whether we like it or not, spells duty."

—Prime Minister Sir Winston Churchill

1
A Difficult Childhood Becomes His Strength
— Russ's Narrative Begins

"Out of the effective remnants of his childhood (are) the hopes of his anticipated adulthood."
— *Erik Erikson*

Russ was reading and relaxing on our front porch, "Well, here I am, a chip off the old block after all. I'm either in my rocking chair on the porch or my recliner chair in front of the TV." He sighed while laying the Desert Sun, our local newspaper, on the glass table top, a bit dusty from the wind-blown sand. He swore he'd never sit on the porch like his Dad did, with nothing to do but rock away the hours and fall asleep in the warmth of a setting sun.

I sat down beside him on my own glossy-white, high-backed rocking chair, made comfortable with blue and white stuffed gingham pillows. "Today, you're as nervous as a cat in a room full of rocking chairs! Tell me, what are you thinking?"

"I can remember the war as though it was yesterday, but I can't remember what I had for breakfast!" Russ reached into his pocket for his wallet and pulled out his little bibelot, his good luck charm from D-Day. For the past 70 years, he still kept it with him, a piece of the parachute he had

Lest We Forget

cut out of his chute when he jumped behind the lines in Normandy. He started rolling the green silk between his fingers. It was a symbol of his appreciation for life.

WWII Veterans are getting too old to attend their own annual reunions of empathizing, mutual understanding, Band of Brothers. Of the few who remained, 2015, over 1800 were dying every day. Their stories will soon be forgotten unless passed on at family reunions. Too often, by the time interest strikes like a bolt of lightning, the one to ask questions from is not there to ask. It is too late.

We were waiting, expecting some of the family to come and visit for our own mini family reunion. It's not easy to coordinate the schedules of our large family because they are busy working, taxiing their own children to school, and attending their extracurricular activities. "That's why you're nervous. You know they want to ask questions about your WWII memories and you're afraid you won't remember some things, because you would just as soon forget."

A Difficult Childhood Becomes His Strength

Francis Russell Snell, born September 21, 1923, was photographed as a bright-eyed baby. Russ drove his tricycle much slower than he did the WWII Army Harley Davidson motorcycle as a messenger between 506 company units. Adventurous six-year-old, Russ is shown sliding down a hill like he would one day glide through the air as a paratrooper.

Lest We Forget

As our porch-pillow-talk continued, Russ reclined and started to rock back and forth. The chair squeaked a bit to keep company with the crackle in his voice. "Those were the days. I had just turned 19, a Senior in High School. New Castle was the only home town I had ever known."

For Russ as an Indiana boy, Home Town America was wandering through cornfields, catching fireflies and tadpoles, chasing butterflies and dragon flies, going to church plays and picnics. While the food was being arranged, all the kids were playing hide and seek or kick the can. For generations his family had gone to Memorial Park to feed the ducks and play baseball. Together during our honeymoon visit, as the October leaves were beginning to change, 1989, Russ and I relived that "Back Home Again in Indiana" memory.

As Russ leaned backward on the rocker runners, he said with a big smile and a little sigh, "Oh, how well I remember jumping bare foot into those huge piles of fallen autumn leaves that had been carefully raked up. The other boys and I went skinny-dipping, jumping into the cold creek."

He paused, "But, I guess I was always too little! I was too short to be on the basketball team and too small to be on the football team." He thought he'd be trampled, toppled, and torn apart by the bigger guys, but like everyone in the State of Indiana, he went to the games and cheered on their teams. Finally, it wasn't enough to just be a

A Difficult Childhood Becomes His Strength

spectator. With their athletic drive and dream to participate, it drove Russ and his brother Tom into joining the New Castle Bowling Team. "Several times we were League Champions in the American Bowling Congress. That was something we did very well."

"Bowling was familiar territory to me because at the age of 15, I had already started setting pins to make some extra money for our family. It was one of the many job opportunities I had taken during and following the Depression."

As he laughed from the fond memory, Russ continued to give details and tell stories about his childhood. "Ducky owned the bowling business. He hired and fired!" When Russ's brother Tom was promoted to manager, Russ got his job in the ice cream corner, which was a lot more fun and tasty! Russ continued, "We could never afford much ice cream, but Ducky said I could have all I wanted and everyone knows how much I still love ice cream!"

Shoehearts Bowling Alley was one of the hangouts for their little town. All alone, before the days of electronics, Russ had to put the pins in the pin-setter by hand. Being in such close range to the pins made it sound like a war zone. It was like playing dodge ball. The pins would go flying past Russ's ears and he was glad for the time he had between players or the next game for a little peace and quiet. "I had to move as fast as the flying pins

Lest We Forget

before the next player would start screaming at me, but I was used to being screamed at. My first job, at nine years of age, was standing on top of a packing crate and washing dishes at Welts Fish Market on 18th Street. Handling those big pans and so many dishes was a lot of work when I was so little! But Welts had the best fish I've ever tasted and I could eat all of it I wanted!"

"I was just thinking about my brother Tom. He was called 'Hoss.' Everyone had nicknames in those days. I was 'Rut.' My brother was always older and always bigger and better looking than I was! He looked just like Cary Grant! I don't know where you heard his nick name was 'Toss,' but maybe someone called him that from his turn at setting pins and having them tossed at him! 'Hoss' was an appropriate nick name, the same as the big guy on Bonanza."

Like every eighteen-year-old guy, Russ was ready to conquer the world, but he didn't know he would be doing it in a world war. He started rocking a little bit more briskly, "I was ready to get through school, get a job and be on my own because my brother and sister were both married and my Dad, had remarried, after Mom died. I had already been working for nine years, so I had no fear of work or getting a job! My plans were to get married to my high school sweetheart, Rosemary. She was popular, sociable and a beautiful red head who loved to dance."

A Difficult Childhood Becomes His Strength

Russ suddenly stopped talking and put the brakes on his rocking chair. It made me wonder why and so I asked, "Did something change that?"

"I was used to working hard and I was also a hard-driving, fun-loving, all-American kid that loved life, a good prank, and the swimming hole. Sometimes friends and I would sneak through the staff door to hide by the stage to watch and not have to pay for a good movie!"

Russ is a quipster and quick to tease, but it seemed like he was avoiding my question. Somewhat troubled, he continued as he leaned forward, "Those movies started with newsreels. They were shocking to me, but some people seemed rather calloused and indifferent, with an attitude and belief that it was Europe's war. It wasn't America's problem. Those troubling newsreels started in 1940 when I was nearly finished with my Junior year in the New Castle High School and I had plans for a fun, but hard-working summer."

2
Before The War, 1940
— The Summer Marjorie was Born

"To be prepared for war is one of the most effective means of preserving peace."
— *President George Washington*

Americans watched the summer newsreels of 1940 as Nazi Germany continued to leave deadly devastation throughout Europe. Russ was watching black and white movies portraying the high-step marching of the massive German army, hearing the chilling chant of the masses "Heil, Hitler," and looking at the map with their progression through Austria, Czechoslovakia, on into Poland, Denmark, Norway, Belgium, France and the Netherlands. The war escalated as helpless nations crumbled under the strength of the German invasion.

That was the summer that I, Marjorie Anne Delafield, was born at the Shannon West Texas Memorial Methodist Hospital, August 19, 1940. Coming from the small town of San Angelo, in the Lone Star State of Texas, I could proudly claim to be a legitimate cow girl! As I grew up, I realized I had another title, "PK." My Dad was a minister and so I was a Preacher's Kid.

Not wanting to interfere with Dad's bible class, Mom sat out in the comfort of their 1936 Chevrolet, instead of suffering on the hard benches

Lest We Forget

in the big three-pole, outdoor tent auditorium! She was in full, progressing labor. Because I was their 2nd child, she knew what to expect, but she didn't realize that after one pregnancy, the next delivery might go more rapidly. Dad closed the service right on time and was immediately rushed right to the car as quickly as possible. He drove directly to the hospital, which happily for Mom, was nearby. Arriving at 9:20 P.M., the delivery room was already surgically laid out for my birth.

The head surgeon, Dr. Kunath, and his wife were expecting the arrival of their own baby and so every shift the nurses awaited her arrival and prepared the delivery room with a new set of sterile instruments. But, when Mother arrived instead, they had no time to waste. The nurses rushed her into the special delivery suite and I was delivered by Dr. Richmond nine minutes after their arrival! Moms own doctor said, "You didn't even give me time to get there." We've laughed at the privileged priority we were given! The doctor announced, "It's a girl!" I can imagine hearing my parents say simultaneously, "She'll be a nurse!"

Mother wanted to become a nurse. Dad had nothing against that except that he saw no need for it because he was so success driven that he did not expect them to have any financial worries and they would live the life of their dreams. She would never have to work outside of their home. Before my dad, Richard, married mother, he took on full

Before The War, 1940

responsibility to be a good husband and provider by owning their first home, his own car, and having a good job. Already that successful, they were married March 5, 1932 when he was twenty-one years old and she was only eighteen.

Cora Delafield is shown holding Marjorie when the family came home from the Shannon West Texas Memorial Hospital, August 29, 1940. Her dad, Richard and brother, Trevor, sit beside them on the back porch steps of their little San Angelo, Texas home. Marjorie Anne Delafield's first birthday photograph was taken, 1941, at Willis Studio, Sweetwater, Texas.

Lest We Forget

By the time I was born, Mom and Dad had changed their views on a lot of things. Dad decided that there were more important things in life than financial success and he gave up his very successful job at the 1st National Bank of San Diego to go to college and become a minister. Still suffering from the effects of The Great Depression, some family members thought he was being irresponsible, but Mom and Dad were united in purpose. Five months after moving into their first purchased home and making a couple hundred dollars of payments and improvements into the house, Richard's step-father Julian McLain bought the home back. He even paid Mother for the curtains she made and all of the plants they had put into the yard, giving them a slight amount of profit!

As soon as Dad found a place for them to live, which happened to be a tiny bedroom in an elderly couples small home, they packed up their belongings and headed off to college. Richard and Cora Delafield pushed everything they could fit into their little Ford Model A Roadster. They filled every nook and cranny, completely behind and all around them, at mother's feet and even on her lap! The Cedar "hope chest" that Richard and her parents had given Cora for graduation was tied onto the top of the rumble seat and they left for college at two o'clock in the morning!

Before The War, 1940

When the young Delafield's started out, it was a very dark moonless night, without even an occasional street light. Crammed and heavily overloaded, Dad was startled to see a bright light that came out of nowhere from a car behind them. That was 1934, the first year police cars had metal-mounted lights on the top of their cars. To the policeman, Mom and Dad must have looked like Bonnie and Clyde with a Cedar chest full of money! "Where are you going?" Surprisingly, Dad's explanation satisfied the cop. Little did Mother know, that would be the first of many times Dad would talk policemen out of giving him tickets. It was also the first of over thirty-five moves during their seventy-year lifetime together!

Another change of their opinion was about women having a college education. Dad regretted that Mom did not become a nurse. He saw it as a noble profession of service, an almost spiritual side to it, a "high-calling" in itself that was also "ministering!" Dad was very proud that while he was in college, Mom received "Certification for Home Nursing," but most of her time was spent selling magazines, ironing or cleaning, and any other little jobs she could find to get Dad through college.

After having a son, Trevor, who they hoped would follow in his dad's footsteps and become a minister, they wanted a daughter to be the nurse that mom was not. It's wonderful to have parents

Lest We Forget

who want their children to have more than they had. Whether it's a better education or more money, it's not a bad thing as long as the goal is to inspire and teach children to work hard and be true to their potential.

Mom and Dad picked up a 10-cent copy of a Life Magazine on the news stand that came out on the actual day of my birth. Pictured on the cover, framed with a bright, red border, was a black and white photograph of a paratrooper with his silk chute opened into a perfect, full circle. The short featured article was entitled, "Army Uses Towers to Train New Parachute Troops." The magazine story tells of plans to train our military, showing pictures of men jumping from platforms and learning to land with a perfect roll. Rather than the original practice of jumping from an airplane, the infantry was now jumping from high towers, sprawling out their free fall in less than graceful positions! Located in Hightstown, New Jersey, this was the beginning of a trial training idea, originally executed from WWI Airplanes, 1929. Little did they know, or I for that matter, that I would marry my paratrooper fifty years later!

I was less than 20 days old when on September 7, 1940, "The Blitz" attacks on England began. For 8 1/2 consecutive months, the relentless, repeated, unmerciful bombings were carried on, including 71 attacks on London alone, destroying over one million homes. During the

Before The War, 1940

period of 57 consecutive months, London was being destroyed, but they would not be demoralized. Over 100 metric tons of high explosives were dropped on the British people, including 16 other cities, primarily Birmingham and Coventry, where their factories of ammunition and tanks were located. The German word for "lightning," this Blitz was the most shocking storm the world had ever known.

America had gone through our involvement in World War I and was still focusing on surviving The Great Depression. It seemed like creating jobs was more important than getting involved in another war. We thought, we hoped, and prayed that what was happening over there would stay over there.

From behind the scenes of Life Magazine's photographs of war depicting the blank, shocked expression of children's faces, Americans attempted to go on with their lives. Homeless British children did not look scared, just blank, because they had become immune to the sound of bombers during the Blitz and the destruction that followed all around them. Hitler was marching across Europe invading, overtaking, overpowering one country after another, leaving behind him devastation, starvation, and fear. There already was a war and we were already in it emotionally, morally, and conscientiously. Those innocent children of England and Europe were already in the war, but so were we. Although we held onto the hope and dream that

Lest We Forget

we were secure from another war because President Franklin Roosevelt promised us that our young men were not going there, we were afraid. How long should America wait? How do we know what is the right thing to do?

England would stand. There had always been an England and there always would be. America tried desperately to believe we had nothing to fear. Auschwitz was simply a name that had no meaning. We were in a denial mode. Excuses, or did Congress know of threats that they were not telling us? Families began to realize that their sons would have to register at draft boards, but with hope it was just for us to be prepared and protected. "It's to defend ourselves." "No fear." "We're not going there."

Some people believed, like my dad, that women shouldn't work, much less be involved in a war. Except for being teachers and nurses, women were told that if they went to college it was just to find a successful man. The belief was that women were better off becoming good wives and mothers rather than to have a paying job. Little did anyone know that this war would change the lives and roles of American women, as well as our young men.

II
AMERICA ENTERS WWII
1941

"These are the times that try men souls . . . the harder the conflict, the more glorious the triumph."

—Thomas Paine

3
How America Responded to Pearl Harbor
— Russ and Family Hear of Attack

"Hawaii calls and my heart's calling too."
— Harry Owens

Hoosiers love their summers with family and friends, gathering for the familiar barbecues that included home-grown corn on the cob and large, fresh sliced beefsteak tomatoes from their gardens. Fortunately for Russ, the summer of 1941 went quickly because he was anxious to get back to school with his classmates and more importantly to finish school. As his Senior year began, it was both exciting and sobering. Students questions were the same as young people have today, wondering where do I go from here and what am I going to do when I graduate?

The world had never seen or been more aware of the destructive power held in the hands of a brutal dictator. That awareness added to the frustration of students facing their graduation. The fear in the hearts of Americans was growing, because we were wondering whether we could remain isolationists. When Russ watched the newsreels, he kept hearing more about being a

Lest We Forget

paratrooper. That service looked appealing and exciting to him.

The year 1941 was a great film year of movies that are still familiar and famous today. The Wolf Man, a classic horror movie, and even Dumbo, with its charming animation, were must-see events. Continuing to be the most recognizable movie was The Maltese Falcon, an all time great classic film. It is still controversial that How Green Was My Valley won Best Movie of the Year, over Citizen Kane, considered by some to be one of the ten best movies, if not the greatest movie of all time!

On December 7, 1941, it was not during a movie or in a newsreel at the theater that American citizens heard of the attack on Pearl Harbor. It was the radio that brought the news. At 2:26 P.M. Eastern Standard Time, NBC broke into Sammy Kaye's music and suspended their National Vespers that night. CBS interrupted the progress of the New York Giants and the Brooklyn Dodgers with a news bulletin, catching the reporter in a moment of silence as he read the ticker that a second attack had occurred (just like on 9-11). As Morse Code reports arrived, Edward R. Murrow gave the news. One station discontinued the New York Philharmonic Program, as this was not a time to enjoy the relaxation and enjoyment of sounds from an orchestra. The serious news spread quickly.

Everyone knew that America would now be at war, and Russ knew that his life was about to

How America Responded to Pearl Harbor

change. He described, "At my dad's, my brother's, and my sister's homes, we were all gathering around our radios." Families across America were sitting in front of their radios, leaning forward, sitting on the edge of the seat of their dining room chairs or over-stuffed sofas, where they had once leaned back and relaxed. All were awaiting the announcement that President Franklin Roosevelt would be speaking to Congress and it would be broadcast in homes across America. Everyone was glued to every word as it came in. The speech lasted only seven minutes.

Firmly and with resolve, the President started to speak, "Yesterday, December 7, 1941, a date which will live in infamy. . ." and he proceeded to declare war against Japan. Within hours, congress voted with agreement and full support. We were thrown into a two-front World War, because only a few days after the Pearl Harbor Attack, Nazi Germany declared war on the United States.

As we talked, Russ let out an audible sigh, "That was all I needed to hear. I knew I needed to prepare for war, to volunteer, and do my part. If I didn't volunteer, I knew I would be drafted." Hawaii called for America to help and Russ's heart was calling him, too. He had to enlist.

During the coming days, Russ started talking to his sister Alice and his brother Tom, sharing with them his interest in being a paratrooper. Their Father had remarried and his brother Tom married

Lest We Forget

Bertha Mae Stevens on February 21, 1942. On March 26, only a month later, his sister tragically and unexpectedly passed away from a severe infection. That was an awful lot for Russ to go through in three short months, giving him such a dreadful sense of loss that he decided his life would be best spent serving his country. He thought his family didn't need him, but his country did.

Russ had such love and respect for his sister Alice that home life wouldn't be the same without her. It was such an indescribable family tragedy to lose Alice, a young and precious person, and the new mom of a beautiful, curly-haired little girl. Born on March 12, 1940, "Kay," had just turned two years old when her mother Alice died.

Twelve days after Alice's death, the first patient with streptococcal septicemia received an injection of Penicillin and all the family believed that Alice would have lived if her infection could have been treated with this new cure. Three years later, at the end of the war, Fleming received the Nobel Prize for the discovery of the life saving antibiotic, which saved the lives of many WWII troops. Ellis Crum was blessed to have his little girl, Mabel Kay as the gift from their short two years of marriage.

Ever since Russ's Mother died when he was nine years old, he felt like he had been kicked around between his Dad's home and various other relatives, and finally to his favorite Aunt Ali and

How America Responded to Pearl Harbor

Uncle Art Biddle's home. They had no children and felt blessed to have Russ in their big, beautiful brick, two-storey home in Lockland, Ohio. They loved him, gave him piano lessons, good clothes and great memories. Russ was being taught the business by helping out in their successful music store in Redding, Ohio, about ten miles away from home. Russ speaks fondly of the loving home he could have had and laughs, "I liked seeing how the other half lived."

Russ's Uncle Art and Aunt Ali asked Thomas, "We'd like your permission to adopt Russ and continue to give him a good home." Russ's father angrily replied, "You're not keeping my son and changing his last name," proceeding to bring Russ home immediately. Shortly afterwards, Russ was sent to live with his sister who was nine years older and her young husband, Ellis, both of whom welcomed him.

It took a lot of courage to make the decision to quit school during his senior year. Russ didn't want to be a burden to his dad or in the way of his newly-wed brother Tom, and young bride, "Bert." Russ thought a lot about the losses he had experienced, not being adopted and the death of his mother and sister. Russ had never felt sorry for himself and decided the most responsible thing for him to do was to get on with his life and prepare for war. That's what many "boys" across America were doing.

Lest We Forget

Russ's friend Don Davis had a car and a good job at Delco Remy in Muncie, Indiana, and so Russ moved there, got a job with his friend and rode with Don to work. He started making tail lights for GM at Delco Remy, all the time waiting, preparing, and planning on going airborne! Knowing that Military Service with the paratroopers would give him $50.00 a month more pay, that gave Russ the extra incentive he needed! It was just a matter of time before he would leave for training to be a 101st Airborne paratrooper, without going into boot camp.

4
Experiencing Pearl Harbor
— Marjorie's Parents Hear About the
Attack on Pearl Harbor
December 7, 1941

"Let us remember that if we suffer tamely a lawless attack upon our liberty, we encourage it, and involve others in our doom."

— *Samuel Adams*

"Pearl Harbor" sounds like an exotic, romantic hide-away! It implies a tucked-away inlet on the island of Oahu, where my parents had been many times during their four years living in the Hawaiian Islands. As missionaries, they sometimes lived in a modest wood shutter home on a pineapple plantation along with the factory workers, because during the years of 1934-1938, it was not the busy, bustling, vacation resort that it has become today. Sometimes it was very difficult for them to find a place to live.

Honolulu, at that time, was already the most populous area and it was a well-known territory that grabbed the imagination back home on the Mainland. The name "Pearl Harbor" plays on the fanciful idea of pearl divers gliding their way deeply into the turquoise, emerald green water, surfacing, cutting open an oyster, and finding the most perfect diamond of a pearl, the diamond of the Islands!

Lest We Forget

The popular lyrics to "Hawaii Calls" was most recognizable from the sheet music as sung by Harry Owens. From the introduction on October 14, 1935, during the short wave radio broadcast originating in the Royal Hawaiian Hotel in Honolulu, the signature song on the program, lasted for decades:

> *"With a melody of love, dear*
> *Across the sea as evening falls;*
> *The surf is booming on the sand*
> *At Waikiki tonight..."*

Back home in the little town of Ramona, California, where the families of Richard and Cora lived, dad's sister Thomasea was dreaming of becoming an opera singer. She performed in school plays, at the Mother's Day program, and was student leader of the music program. In the Music Box Revue she sang, "The Song of the Islands, where skies are calling me, where balmy air and golden moonlight caress the waving palms of Waikiki."

Late afternoon, December 7, 1941, Richard and Cora Delafield were preparing for a nice relaxing evening with friends. It was mother's birthday and the Dittburners had come over to celebrate and enjoy the evening, as well as to have a delicious piece of home-made lemon meringue pie that Mom chose to make, instead of baking herself a cake!

Experiencing Pearl Harbor

Jessie and Dorothy spoiled me because I was born a Texan and they had also been there to celebrate my first birthday. They laughed at my first sentence when Dad asked me, "What do you want to be?"

"Wanabea noise," I innocently replied. I obviously didn't know what it meant when I was taught to say, "a nurse!"

News spreads quickly, but on that evening of celebration my parents were unaware of the horrible news. Although not "in" the war, Americans were realizing the intensity of the war as Hitler marched across Europe. Dad turned the radio on, like Americans were doing across the country to see if there was anything new about the war, when he heard the shocking report.

The heavy wood Philco short-wave Radio/Phonograph sitting on their table top brought the startling, frightening facts that Pearl Harbor had been attacked. My parents first thought, of course, was of dad's brother Arthur, his wife Evelyn, and my two little cousins Corinne and Bobbie who lived in Honolulu. Richard, Cora and their friends immediately prayed for the safety of our family, not knowing that at the time of the attack, his brother was conducting a live, on-air broadcast, "The Voice of Hope" on KGU, Honolulu.

As the bombs fell, the explosions shattered nerves and ships. Arthur would not be distracted and continued to speak. He prayed for the safety of

Lest We Forget

the listeners, talking about the Second Coming of Christ and a new home in heaven. As people in the community listened, they hid in their homes or ran for cover. Until the station went off the air, Arthur was their "voice of hope."

It looked and felt like the end of the world. Right when the crowds thought it was over, there was another bombing. No one knew where it would strike next. On them, at home, or on the mainland? Imagine it, in comparison and similarity to having a relative at the New York Twin Towers on 9-11 when the planes struck, also with repeated attacks.

Aunt Evelyn drew my cousins together. Corinne was only three years, four months and Bobbie was twenty-two months old. Evelyn wondered if they would survive, if she could protect her children and if her husband was still alive. It was hours before he was able to return home. They believed it was an answer to their prayers when he walked through the door. Before their eyes, amidst the eruptions, smoke and flames, Pearl Harbor was being destroyed, but Uncle Arthur made it home exhausted and safe.

After the brave and heroic attempts of the Navy to defend and save lives, a systematic search for survivors and recovery began. Salvage divers worked with zero visibility in dangerous, deep debris-covered water, amidst unexploded bombs, and dreadful remains of bodies. The Japanese Air Force had destroyed 2 battleships, 2 destroyers, and

Experiencing Pearl Harbor

188 aircraft. Two-thousand three hundred and eighty-eight lives were sacrificed and thousands more were injured, helplessly suffered physically, emotionally, and were overwhelmed with fear and horror. Knowing that their own family members were in Honolulu, imagining what it must be like, there was no rest until my parents heard that his brother and family were safe and had returned to California.

The emotional toll on the nerves of freedom-loving people, following the surprise attack on Pearl Harbor, influenced Russ's decision to become a paratrooper. The after effect was experienced again as Russ and I silently walked hand-in-hand across the floating bridge that straddles above the sunken hull of the USS Arizona. The year we were married, 1989, the USS Arizona site became a national historic monument where two million visitors a year walk in respect to honor the dead.

The fallen marines and sailors final resting place has a red velvet rope hanging in front of the strong, solid, impressive marble wall with 1,102 engraved names to honor each man who died. Since then, the ships survivors are allowed the opportunity to be buried with fellow servicemen, their ashes returned by U. S. Navy divers.

Throughout his ministry, Uncle Arthur kept on his desk a large shell of a Japanese bullet that exploded near him. As a memory and symbol of God's protection, Russ also kept his own piece of

Lest We Forget

history and thankfulness for his life being spared. His camouflage cut out piece from the parachute jump in Normandy made it through the whole war as it was transferred from one pocket to another, after one battle to the next, and made it back home to America.

5
Traveling The Trains As The War Begins
— Marjorie's Visit to California

"The war has actually begun. Our brethren are already in the field. Why stand we here idle?"
— *Patrick Henry*

When their work was completed in Sweetwater, Texas, my dad was invited to take three months of classes, from March until May, 1942, at a theological seminary in the nations capital, Washington, D. C. When he talked to his brother, dad found out that Art could attend as well. Having just returned from experiencing the horror of the Pearl Harbor attack, it would be a perfect time for the two brothers to spend some time together. The danger at the beginning of the war and because there would be difficulty finding housing in that area during a war, the men were advised it would be better for their families not to attend. Aunt Evelyn took her two children, Corinne and Bobbie, home to spend time at her Mother's home in San Francisco. My mom went to spend the three months with her parents, the Hanson's, in Ramona, California. Many of our parent's families, both sides of grandparents, aunts, uncles and cousins were there. My dad told friends, "We went to the San Diego Zoo for a family reunion!"

Lest We Forget

Dad went with us on the lengthy train ride from Texas to California before taking his own long railroad trip to Washington, D.C. Richard was planning to study hard, but spend as much valuable time as possible with his brother, who nearly lost his life during the Pearl Harbor attack. At the end of the three months, Grandma Hanson was pretty concerned about mom having to travel alone, clear back to Texas with two small children and so she kept telling Trevor, "Be a little Gentleman and help Mommy with your baby sister, Marjorie."

At the age of eighteen, Cora had moved away from her small home town of Ramona, California, where everyone knew everyone and where all the children went to the same school. Families attended one of the two or three small churches in town, or perhaps one of them one week and another church the following, so the children could be with their friends! The time back home again were three wonderful months for mom to spend seeing her family and friends in the little town where she was born and grew up. Throughout my childhood, we always considered Ramona to be our home because we moved so often. Following my parents marriage, it was not very often that Mom was able to go back to see her family and so the months went by quickly before it was time to get back on the Southern Pacific train, back to our home in Texas.

Traveling The Trains As The War Begins

Children have no fear in the security of their parent's protection, but for Mom, it was with mixed emotions, exciting, and fearful at the same time. She was anxious to see Dad again, concerned about the trip and a war going on, but sad to say good-bye to her family. Mother found enough room to put away the things she would need for the trip, and then we all leaned out the window to wave good-bye to her parents and tearful mother. Standing alone on the depot platform, her parents stood with their arms securely wrapped around each other.

Mother boarded the train alone, except for her two small children, Trevor and myself. We pulled out of the depot around 2:00 P.M. for a rough, winding trip through mountains and deserts for the rest of that day, two nights and arrived back in Texas around 9:00 A.M. the third day. A war was going on and the train was full of young, uniformed military men, primarily sailors because San Diego was a major training ground for the Navy. The servicemen were excited to be going home for a short trip prior to their deployment for war. Like my mom's emotions, servicemen felt the same somber, sad sense that they would be leaving their sweethearts and close family members. The country was united in purpose and the military was patriotic and protective of their citizens. Mother had nothing to fear. They would help her in a second, but she was very cautious and dared not sleep. As the excitement of being on a train full of young

Lest We Forget

servicemen tired us, one by one Trevor and I fell asleep, but Mom did not.

With the youthful voices of men in uniform, it was unlikely she could have slept anyway, but Mom got as comfortable as she could and closed her eyes to rest. With one hand to support Marjorie on her lap and the other arm across Trevor to keep him from sliding off the seat, mother kept both of us within her reach!

She clenched her jaw to hold back a smile as she heard a sailor say to his buddies, "Would you look at that lady. She looks like a mother hen, ready to claw at anyone if they get near one of her chicks!"

Little did he know how descriptively appropriate and accurate his remark was, because we were just leaving the home of her parents poultry ranch, where her father raised chickens and turkeys. She knew how a mother hen would act because as a child, she had been attacked more than once while cleaning out the coops or gathering eggs! She had a scar to prove it. At one time Ramona was the turkey capital of the World and her father Jason Hanson was one of the pioneers of the industry.

Mother had two very sleepless nights, feeling the repetitious wheels across the tracks, and hearing the boisterous sounds of anxious men. Even after the servicemen eventually tired and went off to sleep themselves, mother kept her vigil. As the

Traveling The Trains As The War Begins

morning light shone through the windows, Trevor and I were very early to rise and ready for some of the snacks mother had carefully prepared for us.

No doubt we were quite entertaining to the other passengers around us. They asked where we had been and where we were going. Trevor attempted to sing the song we were trying to learn, "Over the hills and through the woods, to Grandmother's house we go." As his little shadow, I tried to copy in my impossible to understand jabber.

One handsome sailor, in his stiffly starched uniform, asked Trevor, "Well, young man, are you a sailor?"

"No," Trevor assured him in a non-threatening childish voice.

"Do you want to be?"

Very emphatically, Trevor answered, "No."

"Well, how about a soldier? Are you a soldier?"

"No! I'm not a soldier."

Relieved and continuing the questions, the sailor asked, "A paratrooper then?"

"No."

"Oh, you're only a marine."

"No. I'm not."

"Well, then, what are you?" asked the sailor.

"I'm a gentleman."

Quite taken back by a young boys answer, all the other military men were laughing at the sailor

Lest We Forget

for relentlessly pursuing the line of questions and to have it implied, it doesn't always take a gentleman to know one!

Mom quickly stepped in to defend her little boy. Apologetically she explained, "I'm very patriotic, because Trevor's Daddy was in the National Guard. I have a brother who is a sailor, one a marine, and a brother-in-law is in the Air Corp. When we got on the train, my Mother told him to be a little gentleman on the train and help me with his baby sister!"

Mother didn't know then, that her one and a half-year old baby girl Marjorie would marry a WWII 101st Airborne paratrooper!

Traveling The Trains As The War Begins

Left: Uncle David Fletcher, Air Corp, shown with Trevor and Marjorie in Amarillo, Texas. His athletic ability provided him with the opportunity to manage a bowling alley in Ireland, providing recreation for the troops.

Right: Uncle Hardin Hanson, shown being idolized by his niece, Marjorie Delafield. He found it difficult to talk about his six years service in the US Navy. He was original crew member on the USS Doyle Destroyer during 64 hour battle along the Normandy coast.

Lest We Forget

Left: Uncle Alfred Hanson was a Marine, stationed in Honolulu, but completed his service, 1937, prior to the Pearl Harbor attack and America entering WWII.

Right: Aunt Elaine Delafield's husband, Uncle John Murphy, was a US Navy Radarman and Electrical Engineer on the USS Biloxi, during WWII.

III
RENDEZVOUS WITH DESTINY
1942

"Remember our battle-cry and motto, 'Currahee,' it's meaning: 'Standing alone. We stand together.'"
—Colonel R. F. Sink

6
Traveling The Train To Camp Toombs
— Russ's 101st Airborne Enlistment
Rendezvous With Destiny, 1942

"The truth of the matter is that you always know the right thing to do. The hard part is doing it."
— General Norman Schwarzkopf

The thumping sound across Europe's railroads were moving Jews from Austria, Czechoslovakia, and Poland into the ghettos for undisclosed reasons, giving reason enough for the invaded countries to be waiting for the United States' best trained servicemen to arrive. The thump-thud, thump-thud of trains on the tracks across America were also the sounds of war as our finest young men boarded the troop trains and waved to tear-filled new brides, sweethearts, moms, families and friends, standing on the platforms of depots in home towns across America, from every State in the Union. The servicemen leaned back on the hard, crowded seats, their heads pounded to the drum beat of the railroad tracks and their hearts to the rhythm of their own mixed excitement.

It was August 6, 1942 when Russ's enlistment was complete and camp Toombs was ready to accept him as part of the first young group to train. Once the opening for the paratroopers was

Lest We Forget

announced, Russ's three-year-older brother Tom grabbed Russ's bag and threw it into his 1937, four-door gray Chevrolet sedan, and drove "Rut" directly to Fort Benjamin Harrison. It was in familiar territory, just outside of Indianapolis, Indiana, the nearest "Big City," and it was only 50 miles from their home town of New Castle.

    That was the small town where both of them were born, grew up, went to school, and attended the First Christian Church together. "Hoss" was the kind of big brother that Russ needed, because their mother "Bessy" died when they were only nine and twelve years old. Tom had bought Russ a white-wall, wide-tire Schwinn bicycle and Russ had enjoyed learning to drive on his brothers Model A. He also loved every chance he could get to drive Tom's beautiful gray Sedan!

    Russ had said good-bye to his friends from childhood: Don Davis who helped him get a job and taught him how to drive on his $25.00 Model A; his fishing partners, Gene Dickerson, Russ Fisher, and Jack Elmore; working on Model Carbon Airplanes with Everett Lucas; and those many adventurous memories with Harry Young, who went sneaking his grandfather's new Ford out of the garage to drive it around with Russ while Grandfather Young slept; but Russ's one and only brother Tom had always been his best friend!

    It just didn't seem like the right time for advice, to reminisce, to talk about their memories,

Traveling The Train To Camp Toombs

or even the dangers of war. It was a pretty quiet drive to the military base. Russ's anxious, long wait was over. After a brotherly hug, Russ was dropped off at Fort Benjamin Harrison. The recruit enlistment officers only took a couple of days to get Russ aboard his own turn on the train, headed for Toccoa, Georgia. The anticipation of aspiring youth, mingled with the feeling of fear about their unknown future confronted them all. Russ was there in time for the urgent priority to get the paratrooper volunteers started into their vigorous, intense training as soon as possible.

Lest We Forget

Traveling The Train To Camp Toombs

Above: F. Russell Snell prepares to board a Pennsylvania tourist train at the 101st 506 reunion, 1994, similar to, but a more pleasant, less stressful ride than the crowded troop train trip to Toccoa, Georgia for paratrooper training. Left Top: Russ and his brother Tom (on left) happy to be together again, home on furlough during military training, 1941. Left Bottom: After the war, 1945, Tom is shown holding and backing Russ up once again.

7
The Rigors of Paratrooper Training
— Russ's Band of Brothers Earn Their Wings

"Army uses parachutes towers to train new parachute troops..."
— Life Magazine cover photograph, August 19, 1940

Shortly after the trains passed through the familiar, flat cornfields, the Indiana military volunteers were traveling over railroads into the Southern hot, humid, rain drenched Georgia summer. Russ felt all alone among other troops arriving at Camp Toombs. They all lined up for a "free" haircut, stripped down for immunization shots, showers, and were issued army bags full of shorts, socks, boots, pants, and personal items. They were a group of total strangers, but they would become his strong, courageous "Band of Brothers" united in purpose and commitment.

The 101st 506, Screaming Eagles had only been activated since July 20, 1942, a mere two and a half weeks before Russ's enlistment was complete. The legend is that their name was infamously taken from the Civil War Battle of Corinth, whose Eagle screeched its way in symbolic fury, with vigor and hope! The officers had a remarkable short time to design a program that would equal the title and make their men earn the right for being given the

Lest We Forget

$50.00 a month higher pay. Paratroopers would get the money because they deserved it.

Col. Robert F. Sink led the intense plan to shatter the marching record held by the Japanese military, and along with the other officers, their men would have the physical ability to endure anything. The calisthenics would be so fast and furious, the obstacle courses would be so difficult, the steep climb carrying a full pack so strenuous, that the paratroopers physical ability would make it look easy for the 101st Airborne. They would earn the right to be proud and cocky, but they would not be over-publicized as glamor boys. With their spit-mirror-shined boots that were made for fighting, tilted caps and bloused trousers, they would have a natural bounce. It would be their right to boast with a vengeance to be victorious, that no one would protest their pay, but would give homage to their heroic deeds.

To belong to the 101st meant you had to volunteer. That alone showed bravery, dedication, and discipline, an initiative beyond the average. It meant to the awaiting officers that these men were fearless. Anyone who was willing to jump out of a perfectly good airplane was consenting to do whatever it takes to belong to the elite, renowned paratroopers.

If any one of these airborne volunteers thought they would be welcomed and treated distinctly better than other services, they were in

The Rigors of Paratrooper Training

for a startling, rude awakening. There was no room for the shoddy renegade. The roughness and demanding personalities of Major General Maxwell Taylor, Brigadier General Anthony McAuliffe and Col. Bob Sink demanded respect because of their leadership strength that would make the men of the 506 the best of the best.

The men of the 101st were not made up of the blind following the blind. They were made up of brawn and core unsurpassed in boldness, courage, and fearless resolve. The 101st had no history to guide, inspire, or lead them, no history to live up to, but "they had a rendezvous with destiny" and they were determined with strong conviction to keep its rendezvous.

Russ belonged to the original group who made up the very initial beginning of the 101st glorious, elite history. Being among the first to arrive, no barracks or mess hall had been built yet. As the volunteers arrived at Georgia's "Muscle College," they were greeted with a wall of tents, lined between ditches of mud and pot holes. Heading off to find their tents, the guys sank ankle deep into the drenched earth.

"I'll never forget it. I never saw such rain and mud!" Russ shook his head and described being assigned to his bivouac. "There was nothing there but tents, nowhere else to lay our weary bones, except on cots sinking deep into the water-drenched mucky, slushy floor."

Lest We Forget

Finding their assigned lodging was nothing compared to what was in store that night. Intense rain poured over the plowed fields, creating fast-flowing, automatic and unexpected rivers of mud right through every row of over-crowded tents. The word spread from tent to tent, "If anyone needs it, we've got running water over here!"

The Reveille wake-up bugle rooster bellowed to the paratrooper battalion of ducks on parade to start their waddle through the muddy riverbed. That was okay. The mud had not buried them during the night. A little rain wasn't going to kill them or their appetites. They'd make the best of it, but to have their housing called "Camp Toombs," that was going too far. Russ reminded me, "It was our group's protest that convinced the officers to change the name of our regiment from 'Camp Toombs,' to the famous, historical 'Camp Toccoa.'

"It seems like about three months we roughed it in those crowded tents," Russ groaned. The sleeping conditions were tough, the officers tougher, and the paratrooper training was the toughest ever endured. Of all military services, no one had ever imagined anything like the obstacle course that Col. Sink and others created. Col. Sink must have delighted as the men sank into the murk, but just as students love and respect their toughest teachers; the men loved Col. Sink.

The paratroopers were like Olympians, being worked harder than thought possible. From the

The Rigors of Paratrooper Training

ancient Greeks example, they were being trained for war. During the hot, humid summer days, for over 50 torturous minutes, three days a week, Russ described his memory, running Currahee Mountain, which was three miles up and three miles back. That mountain became more challenging as the men ran with the weight of packs on their back, preparing for additional weight when the packs were full. Finally they carried additional supplies, knee packs with loaded, full pockets that altogether weighed almost as much as they did. When the three mile run began, an ambulance followed behind for those who fell cold and unconscious, but as they gained in strength and endurance the 101st could run the six miles in less than 50 minutes. With the spirit of a deer, the 506 became the hardiest physically shaped of any Army Unit.

    Col. Sink knew how to give orders and the men knew how to take them. He drove them to a spirit that would go further, do more, and achieve more than ever imagined. He would strengthen the legs of school boys into muscles of steel! He would expand their lung capacity beyond an opera singer. Their willpower to withstand the tortures of war would deprive them of food, sleep, and water. His American boys became men with energy and endurance never tapped before, to reach for something greater than they normally could. Fortunately, Sink was not as sadistic as some officers were.

Lest We Forget

The best humor comes through human suffering and the paratroopers training was no exception. The 101st had to climb a "pipe ladder" of 12 to 17 logs. Hand-over-hand they were "emulating Darwin's version of our ancestors," perhaps swinging on the original monkey bars for humans! The men thought a monkey's tail would have been mighty handy! Imagine "playing" with huge tree logs and in rapid succession heaving the trunk and lifting them with their legs while lying flat on their backs. When you can laugh at yourself, it doesn't hurt when someone else laughs at you.

The following day of training was worse than the one preceding because the calisthenics lasted longer and the obstacles were more difficult. The men cursed themselves for volunteering. Agonizing in pain by the end of a twelve-hour day, some could no longer make it up a twelve log ladder and would struggle to make their way around it. The troops believed that when the bugle sounded for chow, they wouldn't be able or care to eat. But when the bugle did sound, a single man would find an adrenalin surge strong enough to turn his crawl into a charge to the mess hall, challenging every man to run and make it there ahead of the rest. A big meal is all that was needed to restore and build back their energy for the next day routine to begin all over again.

We went to the Company C. 101st reunion in Scranton, Pennsylvania, 1994. Russ introduced me

The Rigors of Paratrooper Training

to one of the men whose nickname during the war was "Chow Hound Summers." He still lived up to his name by being a great host and planned delicious meals for us all to run to the front of the line for!

No other training location is more recognized than Toccoa, Georgia. Throughout its history, every 101st Airborne soldier has a remarkable story to tell about the toughness of their training. To accustom men to the nauseating smells of war, abscessed wounds and rotting bodies, Easy Co. had to crawl through the stench of hog trails. To get use to the sight of blood and sounds of the suffering, 1st Lt. H. Sabel ordered his men of the 2nd Battalion to throw their knives at piglets, to hear the cries of the tortured. Inflicting cruelty on helpless animals would not be allowed today, but at the time, no sympathy, excuses or exceptions were made. Every man had to take orders or get out. There was no place for weak-spirited men, if they intended on being paratroopers in his battalion.

After a full day of the most intense training, men were pushed even further, beyond all human capability, where their bodies could not take the agonizing muscle cramps, throbbing body aches and blisters any longer. The troops collapsed for a night of sleep to recover. Sometimes they were startled from a deep sleep for a ten to twelve mile night march. After all injuries had been treated and all complaints were done for the day, it was clear

Lest We Forget

that a humble pride for their accomplishments was being earned. Complaining didn't get any 101st Airborne out of a single calisthenics, duty, or exercise. The paratroopers were suddenly aware that they liked all the things they could do. They might as well enjoy it and be proud of what they had achieved before the war would begin.

The organized 101st 506 Airborne were broken down into nine companies, A through I: Able, Baker, Charlie, Dog, Easy, Fox, George, Howe, and Item Companies. There were three Battalions, each of whom had three companies. There was also the Headquarters, Special Unit. Russ for instance, was in the 1st Battalion, Company C, "Charlie," and he thought that turned out to be quite lucky for him on more than one occasion! On one competition for the 3rd Battalion, they were pushed beyond human endurance and some never recovered. Besides individual satisfaction, occasionally the 506 were granted the reward for a chance to go into town. The men competed strenuously to be the ones to earn the prestigious award of a three-day pass. The challenge was a dry-firing, acid test, a rivalry between platoons, companies, and battalions, but then the surprised disappointed paratroopers had to march, rather than ride back to camp following the three day reward for winning.

Russ and I started to read from our copies of reunion scrapbooks from his 101st 506, Company C. annual meeting. Russ said, "I don't remember some

The Rigors of Paratrooper Training

things, but my Currahee book has the best history about our Unit. There are a lot of things I can't remember, but I do remember if you had any fear, men were there one day and gone the next."

It was an opportunity to tell Russ it was OK not to remember. The "Good Lord" must have made us that way! It's kind of like a woman who goes through a difficult or life-threatening labor to deliver a baby. She swears she'll never have another baby, but time heals the pain and she's able to forget the complications and experience the joy of having another beautiful baby! After their life-threatening experiences, the paratroopers would have the reward of saving lives and preserving freedom.

I turned back to Russ, "Do you remember anything else you want to tell us?"

"It was unbelievably tough! Every day we did chin-ups, push-ups, rope climbs, knee-bent, duck-waddle walks, and an obstacle course that we called the 'torture course.' Man, was I in shape!"

As the men persisted through the torturous, almost sadistic program to increase their strength and endurance, they developed rivalry between the platoons, as a way of building their confidence! Every company and battalion competed, knowing that the more they did, the more points they were credited. By the time they left Toccoa, the paratroopers would be better fit than any unit in the U. S. Army. They would have the reputation of

Lest We Forget

being the hardiest and most desirable of any service unit in American history, because only 3 out of 5 completed the program.

Right when the paratroopers thought the preparation could not be any more vigorous, it was. They were sent on a march with actual rations, in weather causing their canteens to freeze. Hungry, dehydrated, and exhausted, during the middle of the night there was a "gas alarm." Fully masked, the march continued. Once they finally found water, a sign marked that it was contaminated with "hawg innards." Returning to camp, their starved bodies were too tired to eat. If they ate they couldn't taste it or they couldn't hold it down. Thinking they were going to die, all the while they were being prepared to live.

Russ remembers the time the 3rd Battalion was sent on ahead for a 120 mile march from Fort Benning to Atlanta in the worst of Georgian weather. The men fell to the ground, knee deep in mud, sleet, and ice, while carrying their bayonets, trench mortars, and machine guns. That was another time by being in the 1st Battalion, Russ escaped an assignment of poor judgment by the commanding officers. Mistakes were made.

Finally the 101st Airborne were ready for the practice parachute jumps from the towers. The men only jumped once in a chute prepared and packed by the professionals. It was followed by hours of practice being spent folding their own parachute,

The Rigors of Paratrooper Training

followed by inspection of their work to see if it was done correctly, and then the men were on their own. The silk parachutes were nicknamed "Cocoon Worms" and felt as comfortable and familiar in their hands as a pair of socks, but Russ knew now why it was so important to do it right and not make a mistake. He recalls the feeling, "If I did it wrong, I risked breaking a leg, my neck, or even losing my life when I had to jump from the plane."

Men knew the tower jump practices were the final stage of learning how, prior to the required five jumps from the C-47. And then they would be pinned with their wings. Marjorie bonded to Russ's thrill, "It must have been as great a feeling or more so, than I felt when receiving my pin as a graduate registered nurse."

The 101st were keenly aware that a paratrooper's job was only 1% jump, 99% marching and fighting, but they had to be able to jump. After completing the training, 6% failed to qualify for the jump from the plane. Russ remarked, "I was next to a man who wouldn't jump out of the plane. They pulled him out of the line, moved him to another service, and we never saw him again."

Airborne men expressed how jumping felt: "Like my heart was in my mouth, a breath-taking void, like galloping butterflies, a drunken family reunion within." But holding that powerful harness in their hand was a great symbol of strength, being in charge of their own destiny. Parachuting was a

Lest We Forget

beautiful feeling, but Russ decided that someday he'd rather be a pilot than jump from a plane.

Within three hours, the 101st 506, in remarkable precision, control and accuracy, jumped from the planes over Lawson Field, Fort Benning. Again, they were record breakers: 1750 jumps, ten men a minute. The song, "I've got that wonderful, worrisome feeling," was certainly true when the paratroopers, completed the requirements to receive the ultimate reward. Those who received their airborne wings pin had survived the intense wounded training of blistered, exhausted, wounded bodies that separated the men from the boys.

After multiple mock jumps from the towers and their five required full parachute airplane jumps, the paratroopers were dressed in their finest, smartly creased pants, and mirror-polished boots, to stand before their officers at Fort Benning. Being pinned with their wings was truly that wonderful, very satisfied, proud, but worrisome feeling, knowing the next phase would be to war. Where and what was next?

The Rigors of Paratrooper Training

F. Russell Snell (above left) grasps his pack, with straps to his back, knee pads, and in position for a practice jump, Fort Benning, Georgia, 1941. Also shown, with his boots on the ground, Russ has that familiar parachute on his back.

A Headquarters Memorandum was presented to the 506 Parachute Infantry Regiment from Colonel R. F. Sink, Commander, December 18, 1942:

> You have now become qualified parachutists, and wear wings of the parachute soldier. You are a member of one of the finest regiments in the United States Army and consequently the world.
>
> You are about to go on furlough, into the homes of relatives or of friends. I feel that

Lest We Forget

I should remind you of certain things that are expected of you – not only while on furlough, but also a creed by which you are expected to govern your life and your actions:

1. You must keep in mind that first you are a soldier in the Army of the United States; that you are a parachutist, the elite of this Army, and finally that you are a member of the 506th Parachute Infantry.
2. You must walk with pride and with military bearing.
3. You must be careful of your personal appearance, keeping your uniform neat at all times.
4. You must do nothing to bring discredit upon the Army, Parachute Troops, or this Regiment.
5. Remember our battle-cry and motto, "Currahee," it's meaning: "Standing Alone. We stand together."

The Regiment Commander desires that you convey to the members of your family his personal greetings.

Signed, R. F. Sink, Colonel, 506th Parachute Infantry Commanding Officer.

The Rigors of Paratrooper Training

Without any doubt the men were prepared. Col. Sink had trained his men to have the right in a humble way to boast, knowing the world would pay homage to the deeds and heroism of those who survived and succeeded in their mission. Those who would die, would do so quietly, with the living to carry on the principles and values of their job well done. These paratroopers would have a long-lasting legacy and deserve the respect, admiration, and honor of being the Greatest Generation, the greatest military forces for freedom that the world had ever known.

IV
FROM FURLOUGH AND FAREWELLS TO FREEDOM

"I thank God you are here. From the bottom of my heart I wish you all good fortune."

—Prime Minister Sir Winston Churchill

8
Furlough Home With the Family
— Russ Goes Back Home Again to Indiana

"You never really leave a place you love – you take part of it with you – leaving part of you behind."
— *Unknown*

Russ left his New Castle, Indiana home in August, 1941, and returned for the first time on a short furlough the middle of December. In four brief disciplined months he had earned his wings following the hard-driving, strict training that took him from being just an Indiana country kid to a man, nineteen years of age. At that family reunion, Russ's step-cousin Phil Mark took 8mm Kodak movies of their gathering. Watching the movies years later, one would think that everyone was celebrating the end of the war. The family joyfully celebrated the return visit of Russ and his brother. During Tom's physical examination he was diagnosed with flat feet and would not be able to go into combat. Instead, he was trained as a Military Police, MP. No one except the two brothers had a realistic idea of what was in store for them when they would leave for war.

Time flew by while visiting family and being surrounded by the familiarity and comfort of home. When Russ returned to "stand alone, yet stand together" with his Company C Band of Brothers, he

Lest We Forget

was back in "Bama" country. They squeezed in one last practice jump, but this time with their rifles, guns and supplies. The rifles had become such a part of them. They knew their equipment and supplies like the back of their hand. Russ said, "I could take my rifle apart and put it back together again with my eyes closed." They did not know from one day until the next what, where, or when to expect departure. Their time in Alabama was very short.

"Pack 'em up. We're movin'," the order came. Following a quick, good-bye to that State, the 506 were off to North Carolina. Camp Mackall was very large compared to the far off primitive, torturous training fields where they started. The paratroopers settled into impressive barracks where everything was organized and ran accurate as a military clock. The men were exposed to the best dining facilities in a brand new comfortable great mess hall with quality ware instead of their canteens. While enjoying delicious meals, they were entertained with modern Juke Boxes playing popular songs of the day, like Mack the Knife!

Furlough Home With the Family

Shortly after volunteering to become a 101st Airborne, Russ earned a few trips into Atlanta, Georgia where he posed for some professional studio photographs, including what appears to be "fly me to the moon, to let me play among the stars," but was actually from the period song Mack the Knife.

There was no let up though. When the 506 started their instructions, they were ground breakers. Teaching paratroopers was based on trial and error, sometimes running them into the ground, but now there had been enough time to build facilities, build character, and build a better training program. From experience, it became known and understood what was most important, that within reason, the marching marathons did build muscles of steel and that successful

Lest We Forget

maneuvers were based on progressive additions of weight, with bayonets, equipment and supplies.

Once fearful and trembling from the 250 foot towers, the airborne jumps were replaced with courageous parachuting from C-47s. Russ's flights created a love for flying, as he flew over the peaceful fields of North Carolina and saw the beauty of the countryside above Sturgis Airfield in Kentucky. He renewed his dream to become a pilot someday.

The comfort and pleasures of being in improved facilities had just begun to sink in. Sound nights of sleep, generous portions of fried chicken, and opportunities to dance with the WACS, Women's Auxiliary Corps, abruptly came to a halt when suddenly, in the middle of the night, the men were rudely awakened. They were off again, and back to troop tents! The Unit Cartoonist called it "Truck Jumps," but the guys decided even that was a nice break from jumping out of planes. The men quickly discovered what was in store and it wasn't anything as easy as parachuting.

It was the time when they were in the midst of what would probably be their last practice mission, the calm before the storm, you might say. It was a top secret mission into an imaginary DZ and it seemed like every American resident was out watching. Were they the "designated enemy?" While the paratroopers were figuring it out, they were in the throw of combat, climbing, sliding, hiding, advancing, and running into unexpected circum-

Furlough Home With the Family

stances. As they attacked, the situation changed, with the other battalion of troops being the possible enemy. This was as much like reality as it would ever be. While enduring lacerations and bruises, they ran out of supplies and there was no time or place to sleep. Their canteens were empty and they were forbidden to fill them when they arrived at a "contaminated" passing stream. The men were praying for relief, wanting to fly again or have the trucks pick them up and take them back to their tents to rest. Shouldn't they have a little more of that R&R, one last chance for enjoyment before being sent to war? Maybe even a little wine, women, and song would be appropriate because this was more than enough to drive you to drink. They wanted any kind of relief from the stress of the unknown in this gruesome, fake mission.

Finally when relief did come, they realized how tired of training they were. It would be better to know their fate than face the unknown any longer. Another practice maneuver was like having a tree limb cut off when you're out at the end of it. They were all at the end of their pretend rope and just wanted to get in there and get it over with. The troops were ready. Please, no more games and playing war. They were ready for the real battle. When would they be rescued from another trial run? No longer wanting a break or the comfort of fancy barracks, they wanted to fulfill their mission, their destiny.

Lest We Forget

    Like their moms, sisters, wives, and girlfriends back home, the men found the greatest relief from stress, was by cleaning! They scrubbed floors until the pattern was worn off the wood. Like a white-knuckled carpet-layer, they were on their hands and knees, scrubbing, waxing, polishing, and house-cleaning with a vengeance. Their boots and weapons looked like new. They couldn't pack and unpack their supplies another single time.

    Beyond rumor, word finally came to march to the trains where the unknown presided. Their march was a wonder-breaking, record-breaking phenomenon into where? Their expectations grew. Excitement overwhelmed them and with the height of anticipation that the majority of men had never experienced before, they were off! The 101st Airborne were headed to America's largest and the world's most famous city, New York, New York, that wonderful town.

Furlough Home With the Family

The first time F. Russell Snell was able to return home after joining the 101st was when he successfully completed his five airplane jumps and received his Wings Badge. At this reunion, shortly before going to England prior to D-Day, he was standing in front of his brother Tom Snell's car, in front of their home, and with his dad, Thomas Boliver Snell, Sr.

9
Boarding the SS Samaria
— Russ Becomes Homesick and Seasick

"Yea, though I sail 'mid the thunders and tempests of life, I shall dread no danger for Thou art with me: Thy love and Thy care they shelter me."
— *Captain J. Rogers*

It was a rude awakening when the men realized that they were going directly to board the ship without any time to party or do any sight-seeing. Most of the men, including Russ, had never seen New York before. Disappointed, but not disheartened, the paratroopers headed by ferry to the SS Samaria awaiting them in the New York Harbor. The men climbed aboard and crammed into an overcrowded spot on the deck side with the best view of the impressive city skyline. As the anchors lifted, the small tug boats tugged on their heart strings and pulled them through the harbor. It seemed that the pilot masterfully dodged U-Boats and kept from heading directly forward into other ships. The mighty ship Samaria, streamed past Ellis Island and the Statue of Liberty. The troops knew that as the great city faded into the far distance, there were American citizens standing along the shoreline and on the docks, waving their fond, emotional, proud farewells. The paratroopers responded by courageously waving a good-bye to

Lest We Forget

everyone who represented to them their own mom, dad, brothers, sisters, wife, or sweetheart back home. Knowing their own family and friends would have been there for them if they could, the thought brought undeniable, unashamed tears to their eyes and a huge lump in their throat.

Representing what they were leaving to defend, Lady Liberty held up the torch of freedom in her outstretched arm. There was no looking back now. The historic statue was unveiled and dedicated to commemorate the alliance between the United States and France during the American Revolution. Without the French influence, America may have been defeated by Great Britain. Now, the forward looking Paratroopers were leaving American shores to preserve our freedom and that of England and Europe.

Freedom was being threatened again in the country where my grandfather Edgar Delafield came from. The same year he came through Ellis Island as an emigrant, 1903, the meaningful bronze inscription for freedom-loving people around the world was posted on the Statue. I said, "Russ, it brings tears to my eyes thinking how emotional it was to leave your homeland and go off to war. It makes me realize how the grandfather I never met must have felt to leave his country and family. I have a connection to your leaving New York and going to Liverpool, because my Grandfather left Liverpool and came to New York.

Boarding the SS Samaria

"Grandfather Delafield was a courageous stranger in a new land, where he knew no one, but met, fell in love, and married my grandmother, Emily Tyne. She was quite a charming, proper, but strong little lady who was brought up with her sister in a New York orphanage. They were taught good principles and values; but hardships left them with little knowledge of their background. Grandma was even unsure of her exact date of birth. She thought quite certainly that she was 50% English and 50% German: the two countries who were now at war.

"Before America's involvement, my Grandmother Hanson called Mother one day and said, 'Cora, I'm very worried and concerned about the escalating threat of war.' It took Mom a lot of coaxing before Grandma told her, 'I'm afraid that because your father-in-law came from England, his son Richard will be considered British and they will draft him to go and fight for England and he may get killed. That would leave you with two small children.'

"Russ, he didn't have to do that for his dad, because you fought for him. You packed your American parachute to fight for England, but you did it for my dad, and for me. You packed our chutes."

Like a stalwart fortress of strength, Ellis Island stood as a solid rock with the dynamic phrase on the magnanimous statue, The Goddess of

Lest We Forget

Freedom. Written by Emma Lazurus, the words fittingly depict the yearning desire of every paratrooper as they left their homeland:

"Give me your tired, your poor, your huddled masses yearning to breathe free. The wretched refuse of your teaming shore. Send these, the homeless, tempest tossed to me."

The paratroopers sailed on September 5, 1943. Most men were still leaning on the rails as the sun set slowly into the horizon until there was no sight of land left, but every 101st Airborne had a firm hand in his pocket, securing the pass that had been issued. Each card had an assigned berth for their own specific spot to sleep aboard the ship for their long Atlantic trip to Europe. The men thought the most unfortunate sleeping assignment was up on deck, but those who realized they were most prone to sea sickness would gladly have traded. The airplane flying 101st Airborne, who ended up in the belly of the ship, had no concept of the seriousness of seasickness during the rough sea storms at night.

Besides their assigned sleeping quarters, the pass had a number for their mess tables. One card read, "Keep this Card. Sleeping Quarters No. 3, 240. Mess Table: Third Sitting, P2E. This card must be retained and produced when necessary. It must not be changed without the Chief Deck Stewards permission."

Boarding the SS Samaria

The guys were looking forward to the ships chow line and expecting delicious meals. After marching, loading, and working all day without eating, it was disappointing to find out that their food had to be rationed. When groups were called for their turn to mess hall, the smell of oily lard and stacks of food proved to taste even more disgusting and nauseating than it looked. Once they saw and smelled the food it didn't really matter anymore because they realized they couldn't keep anything down anyway. While up on deck they felt fine, but down below in the deep hole of the dining room or in their crammed quarters, their stomachs were cramping and paratroopers were getting sick. Now they knew why it was called "mess hall."

To make matters worse, Russ was assigned KP (Kitchen Patrol) duty, which seemed to him like the worst part of his entire torturous military training. Memories of KP confirmed in his mind he would never go on a cruise and potatoes would not be a staple in his diet. He could only wish and pray for a glass-smooth sea. Russ became deathly seasick and thanked God endlessly for his sister Alice, who talked him out of joining the Navy when he entertained that idea. Hours on end he peeled potatoes. That meant skipping many meals as he heaved on an empty stomach. I think that's why to this day, he can live happily without ever eating or seeing another potato! He only eats them because I fix them. I have such a difficult time remembering

Lest We Forget

not to buy them because I love potatoes in every way they can possibly be prepared: boiled, baked, casseroles, fried, mashed, and salads. The more I get, the more I want. The fewer Russ gets, the happier he is.

Never again in his life would Russ volunteer for KP duty. He was OK as long as he didn't have to do the preparation or cooking. Before we got married he said, "You make the mess, I'll clean it up." That seemed like a fair trade for me. After I have prepared and served the meal, as soon as we or our company are finished eating, Russ starts to clear the table so we can get to the dessert. I've often said, "The only reason Russ eats is for the dessert." When we go to a family get together, he always checks out what the desserts are so that he can leave enough room in his stomach to have as much dessert as he can eat and he'll always ask if there is any ice cream to put on top!

Boarding the SS Samaria

The SS Samaria became a WWII troop carrier. Russ was among the 101st, 506 transported to England on this ship. (Appreciation, 1942 Vintage Postcards)

Out on the endless ocean, how dark is pitch? There was nothing out there to see. The only hope left was confidence in themselves and looking up at the stars when the sky was clear enough to dream of a more optimistic future. That's when the paratroopers decided to lighten the mood and came up with the idea of a talent show. Bob Hope was not on board. If he could have been, he would have drastically improved on the talent, but not their attitude. In between their laughter, an officer

Lest We Forget

ordered some calisthenics or rifle checks and then the troops went right back to singing a familiar song or demanding a solo by one of the men. It helped them get over and forget their seasickness. The paratroopers came up with a few gambling games and made bets on their future. That seemed pretty sobering, knowing some would live and many would die.

Considering that they were sailing the mighty, rough Atlantic ocean, the paratroopers had ten days of pretty good weather. Maybe the ocean just felt calmer because they were getting use to it or knew they were nearing England, the calm before the storm, the smooth sailing before facing the rough waters ahead in battle. Everyone heard the yell, "Land Ho!" This time the troops were not leaning on the rails waving good-bye, or sick to their stomach heaving over them, they were holding onto the rails, looking for land. It was Ireland. Slowly past the green fields of the Emerald Isle, the ship finally docked at a pier in Liverpool.

10
From Liverpool to Littlecote
— Russ in the Estate Barn

*"Let us then be up and doing with a heart for any fate:
Still Achieving, still pursuing, learn to labor and to
wait."*
— *Henry Wadsworth Longfellow*

The British were waiting. Not realizing the value and importance of supplies for themselves, the troops started throwing their candy, cigarettes, and gum to the welcoming crowd. It seemed like the right thing to do at the time, not realizing that those things would have meant so much to them in the future. It would not have been a selfish gesture to keep the objects for themselves. The paratroopers were already endeared by the people of England because the troops brought them hope and encouragement. There's strength in numbers.

With their jump boots back on, the men lined up for debarkation. Every one of the 506 marched down those gang planks with determination and resolve, through the streets of Liverpool to the waiting truck transportation. The men were waving a reassuring hand to England's citizens lining the streets. Surprisingly, the British could still smile and wave back. Despite representing hope amidst the destruction, as the sky darkened into night, the troops realized how

Lest We Forget

emotionally and physically exhausting the trip was. With unsure sea legs, they were ready to collapse on dry land, September 15, 1943. The airborne had escaped another seasick, confined night on the ship.

    While some wondered if the cottages looked like the homes of ancestors who immigrated to America, others remembered what they had only heard, read, or learned about famous, favorite, great poets and authors of England: Walter Raleigh, John Bunyan, Chaucer, and of course Shakespeare. While riding past rolling green countryside fields and witnessing the contrast of hundreds of small, shattered homes ruined during the blitz, the paratroopers were there to restore and renew hope to England and the world.

    Being in Battalion 1, Company C, Russ headed to Littlecote, their new camp. It was the famous English Estate of Sir William and Lady Wills. Some paratroopers were fortunate enough to be housed in the home. Russ landed up in the barn! Whether estate or barn, the Americans knew why they were there. The former Red-Coat, Blue-Coat military Revolutionary War against England was now fighting together for them. It took little time for the people of both countries to adjust their thinking and to unlearn their misconceptions. The Yanks informality was as welcome to the Brits as the formality of the Brits was welcome to the paratroopers!

From Liverpool to Littlecote

While Russ awaited the Normandy Invasion, he was staying in the barn of The Ramsbury, Littlecote English Estate where Col. Robert F. Sink was welcomed to set up headquarters. Following the invasion into France, Col. Sink set up new headquarters at this farmhouse. (Photograph courtesy of Nichole Bromme)

The officers slept in the elegant estate. Most of Russ's 506, Charlie Company ended up with him in the Ramsbury barn with straw for a bed. If it was good enough for baby Jesus, it was good enough for them! June, 1999, the town of Ramsbury still remembered the sacrifice of the paratroopers and realized, lest we forget, that they had no significant expression of the history of the 506 paratroopers stationed there. An impressive memorial plaque was erected as part of a lasting memory at the

Lest We Forget

location where Russ spent one year of his life waiting for the D-Day invasion.

All of the paratroopers who drank found that beer in London (for the lucky ones who got their day pass first), was envied by those waiting their turn. They were told that the mild malt and bitter ale was not so bad after all, sympathizing for the others' misfortune. Once the others got their chance, they found the bragging right was over-played and exaggerated! Drinking became less important than the time and frequency during popular trips into Swindon and Marlboro. Having time with the WAAF's, continuously arriving at the airport, was the best time the 101st had spent since first activated. As Russ recalls, "We had a good time, but all the troops had been taught, warned, and well-educated about the dangers of sexually transmitted diseases and that we had a standard of values to uphold. We were warned not to get involved with the Picadilly Commados." Perhaps Russ also thought about the job his big brother had to do as a Military Police!

American family values and language customs during the 1940s were based more on strictness, respect for women, and honoring their elders. Children were to be seen and not heard and so when Russ and I watched the Band of Brothers video series, I did not believe the servicemen swore as much as portrayed. But many of the men had learned to as a means of showing others they were

From Liverpool to Littlecote

not afraid to be bold and express themselves. It made them feel independent and free. As long as it was done without losing their temper or being disrespectful, cursing was a way of letting go of anger and frustration at the things the men had to do, found it difficult to do, or were ordered to do. Russ didn't swear except when he said, "Blow it out your puckered vent!"

One day Russ's veteran golf friend came to our home and had taken a number of drinks before arriving. When he started to curse profanely, Russ led him out the door and back to his golf cart. Russ apologized to me and the next day said to the man, "Yesterday you were out of place. No one curses like that in my home or in front of my wife. You are not welcome back unless you can promise that you will not drink before you visit or speak that way in front of my wife."

By standing up for me and demanding respect, Russ had confirmed a lasting friendship between them. He came back one day with a card punched with various size holes to ring-size Russ's finger. Russ thought it was just for the fun of it, from something the man had found at a garage sale! Six weeks later a FedEx truck pulled up to our door with an impressive gift, an expensive accurately engraved ring with Russ's initials, his full 101st history as a WWII Airborne, with Wings, Screaming Eagle, Purple Heart, and Oak Leaf cluster recipient.

Lest We Forget

The paratroopers rigorous training in England continued for an entire year while awaiting the Normandy Invasion. That was enough time back home in America, at Camp Toccoa, to train replacements for the 101st Airborne, because the officers knew there would be massive loss of lives once the invasion of Normandy took place. The Littlecote Estate became the regimental Headquarters and the rest of the regiment occupied the villages around it. The troops were scattered all the way from Ramsbuy, Swindon, Froxfield, Chiseldon, to Aldbourne, and Chilton Foliat.

Some troops were dug in at Aldbourne, a quiet little five-pub town in Wiltshire, far from the luxuries of the Ramsbury Estate or London. While waiting for their assignment, every paratrooper was constantly being reminded of what was ahead, with continued daily calisthenics to maintain their strength, will-power and focus. Through the dead of winter, the little tar-papered thatch cottages became as welcome and inviting to young homesick paratroopers as the warmth around a fireplace on a winter night back home in Indiana.

As far away as Swindon, the troops continued their hopes of passing time with a little hilarity and merry-making, but were constantly being faced with blackouts, closed pubs, and bombing reminders of the pending war. Realizing there was a big chance not to survive the Normandy invasion, the paratroopers were very generous with

From Liverpool to Littlecote

their money to pay for taxi transportation. One taxi service was known to have "retired" at least five of their cab drivers with enough money to acquire an estate of their own, from the proceeds and tips given by the 101st Airborne! What else was there to do with their money? They'd probably never live to be able to use it, but Russ wisely saw the value in sending some money home to help his family and buy his little two-year-old niece Mabel Kay a few U.S. Savings Bonds. Following the death of his sister, this was one way he found to honor Alice and spend some of his money. Isn't that one reason he joined the paratroopers, to make $50.00 a month more than other services?

Lest We Forget

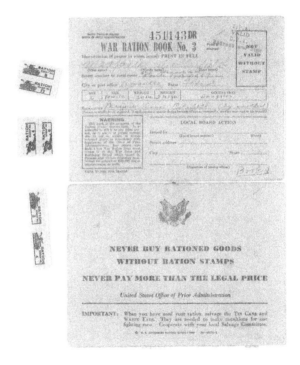

From Liverpool to Littlecote

On reverse: F. Russell Snell's little two-year-old niece, Mabel Kay Crum, is shown with Russ shortly before he left for England. Like Marjorie A. Delafield, she was also born 1940. Russ bought and gave Kay some of his War Bonds. At that time families, including the children, were given war ration books and stamps, as shown of one that belonged to Marjorie at that age.

Below: Detail of the war ration stamps, showing military tanks.

Camp Mackall's boxing team was revived and the troops played American football instead of Rugby in a country that played Cricket instead of baseball. It helped to keep the Americans in touch with their homeland, "to preserve a semblance of the good old U. S. A. and keep everyone happy." But there was a constant reminder of the pending war when called for those simulated jumps. The

Lest We Forget

efficient, unexpected record-breaking moments came and paratroopers could quickly be in their jump clothes and full gear for another practice run, calisthenics or obstacle courses created in a new country that included new and different obstacles. Awakened to the sound of bugles, they never knew when the "real" call would occur.

It was across the beautiful English countryside, but it seemed the compass was as confused as they were to directions. With scarred bodies, torn skin and trousers, everything seemed against the paratroopers once again during another practice routine. The weather reminded Russ of the mud running through their troop tents back at Camp Toombs (before name change to Camp Toccoa). About that same time, my mother took a photograph of my brother Trevor and I, playing in the rain drenched back yard of our Amarillo, Texas home, 1943. While I was having fun playing in the mud, Russ was suffering in the mud, training to fight for the dignity of mankind. The troops unshaven, forlorn faces were covered with mud from head to toe back in Georgia and again, there in England. With aches, blistered and bruised bodies, they were a painful "bloody mess." The 101st were absolutely sure "combat" wouldn't be this bad.

They had no idea.

From Liverpool to Littlecote

While F. Russell Snell crawled through mud trenches during WWII, Trevor and Marjorie Delafield were playing in the mud. When Russ was under medical care following his injuries, Marjorie wore her white pinafore play dress uniform pretending she was a nurse. Her brother Trevor and unidentified neighbor boy are shown wearing their helmets, carrying play guns.

11
The Famous Formidable Four
— Russ Stands Beside
Eisenhower, Churchill, Bradley and Montgomery

"The 101st Airborne Division...has no history, but it has a rendezvous with destiny."
— General William C. Lee, August 19, 1942

"The English Bull Dog," "Ike," "Bradley," and "Monty," became the endearing words paratroopers used to describe the famous formidable four men who would lead them. First it was Montgomery who wanted to meet his troops, but no more than they wanted to see him. He was slight, spry, sky blue-eyed, and scrutinizing as he walked among the rows of men. As thorough as one can be, he liked what he saw and let them know it by stating with conviction there was no doubt the Germans would be crushed. He knew the paratroopers would not fail after seeing the strength, organization and ability of the best-prepared military force in the world's history.

Once the fog began to lift, with a break in the terrible conditions, General Dwight D. Eisenhower agreed with Field Marshall B. L. Montgomery that the men were as prepared as humanly possible. From attention, inspection, and then to break rank, hundreds of American soldiers charged toward the jeep where General Eisenhower stood beside Prime

Lest We Forget

Minister Winston Churchill. It surprised the troops to see an unexpected bare head, quite apparent without Churchill's familiar, formal top hat! The men immediately recognized the form and faces of four great men being among them; Churchill, Eisenhower, Montgomery, and Bradley.

When the cheering was over, order was regained in preparation for the full, more complete inspection. For a whole week, the entire American outfit aimed for perfection, because they knew there would be this dress rehearsal to show the initiative, spirit, and bold courage of the 101st, 506. The men vowed with determination not to disappoint and they didn't.

"Russ, you've said so many times, that you were close enough to rub shoulders with Churchill, Eisenhower, Bradley, and Montgomery. How did you do that?," I asked my own formidable fifth man!

Those were days imbedded in Russ's mind that he would never forget. He said, "It was a bit like 'luck of the draw.' Col. Sink made the decision to choose the 1st Battalion, to appear fully prepared and dressed for the impressive ground inspection. Those four men walked in front of my row and I could have shaken their hand."

Russ and his fellow Company C men of the entire 1st Battalion, wearing their dress uniform, stood at attention in front of the beautifully draped silk parachutes of red, white, and blue American colors decorating the grandstand. The C-47

The Famous Formidable Four

Douglas aircraft roared up their engines and taxied down the runway. Many planes were pulling the great, necessary gliders which would be filled with heavy equipment.

The other Battalions, wearing their full gear and combat uniform, were assigned to C-47 planes for a live parachute jump. The 1st Battalion had marched, been inspected, and stood with perfect, extraordinary ability and efficiency. It was matched with the coordination and skill of the 2nd and 3rd Battalion, performing precisely as if in active service.

Like soaring eagles, the paratroopers swept into a beautiful blue sky, swooping down in a great green mass of roaring, thunderous, army-camouflaged airplanes. The great migrating flock of planes flew in perfect formation. Hundreds of broad-winged massive, manufactured C-47 birds filled the sky. Proceeding toward the door, hook after hook on the static line, the Screaming Eagle paratroopers made their precisely timed, flying leaps. Behind them were descending jeeps, anti-tank guns, hospital supplies, rations, bulldozers, and trailers landing from within the belly of the gliders.

Loaded with their heavy equipment, hundreds of paratroopers filled the sky and headed toward the ground as if lightning tumbling earth bound. Their expert exhibition of speed and precision was miraculous. It didn't matter who did

Lest We Forget

what, because everyone was equally prepared for the most impressive, flawless, and magnificently performed demonstration. It was executed without a glitch just as the headquarter officers had planned. Indeed, masses of men tumbled through the air in a masterful, memorable display. It was a proud moment for the leaders to join their commanding officers on the stage. This is exactly how they planned to do it on D-day.

England's Prime Minster Churchill was the first one to ever inspect an all-American military force on his own soil. He spoke to the men, "testifying to your belief in all those great phrases embodied in the American constitution. I thank God you are here. From the bottom of my heart I wish you all good fortune and success."

The Prime Minister dangled his unlit cigar between the wry, smile on his lips. What he had just seen was so remarkable, he asked for a closer inspection of the equipment. Back in the jeep, he sped towards the glider pilots who ended up having their own private inspection. Imagine their surprise at seeing Prime Minister Churchill crawling into a glider! The paratroopers were relieved with the success of the demonstration maneuvers and gave some relaxed, over-heard comments. Towards their Chief Officers, one of the men said, "I'll be damned, don't he ever go out without his cigar?" Another one said, "Ike looks like a pretty good ol' Joe, don't he!"

The Famous Formidable Four

One paratrooper said, "Ain't Bradley a little guy though!"

Fortunately there were some things the Generals and Prime Minister didn't see or hear. The men excused it as just "nerves." It would never happen in real combat! Or, would it? One of the men ran with his arms overloaded with equipment, desperately and unsuccessfully trying to keep his pants on. During the jump his suspenders snapped and every few yards he fell face first into the dirt, struggling to recapture his composure and his pants. He ran a few more yards, falling again and repeating the process.

Another man couldn't get out of his harness quickly enough and ran off dragging the awkward, yet light weight eleven pound silk parachute behind him! Then there was a clumsy clown who had never jumped with an M3 rifle before and decided to dismantle it. He "never did get the damn thing back together again!"

The men needed a good laugh after the intense preparation and performance day of inspection. Russ said, "We were too busy in training and in combat to kid around very much," but I knew him well enough to know that Russ's dry humor and quick application of circumstances would have made him lighthearted on many occasions.

Before exhaustion and starvation set in, the paratroopers were off to mess hall and a much

Lest We Forget

needed night of sleep. Whether it was word of mouth, a gut feeling, or lapse of time being in England for a year, the men knew that the time was near. It wouldn't be much longer for sure. On June 4, 1944, there was a significant increase of attendance at the Protestant, Catholic, and Jewish services and some men asked for personal time with the chaplain. Some men gathered in prayer or were seen pulling out to read the small size New Testament tucked away in their pocket.

12
The Beginning of the End of WWII?
— Russ, the C-47, the Uniforms

"Now this is not the end. It is not even the beginning of the end. But it is, perhaps the end of the beginning."
  — Prime Minister Sir Winston Churchill

After one year and ten months of training and preparation, Russ was suddenly awakened in the middle of the night. The expected high-tension reason was not just another dry-run, right? It had to be the real thing, but while trying to figure out the purpose and objective, the 506 were told to secure a specific graveyard where the enemy was dug in. "Go in there and flush him out with whatever means necessary," one of the officers ordered, thinking one more practice could make a difference.

"Giving us shovels instead of guns this time?," one paratrooper yelled, relieving the pressure and tension.

On June 5, 1944, Supreme Commander of the Allied Expeditionary Force, General Dwight D. Eisenhower spoke to his men. Without knowing it was the eve of D-Day, Russ listened to the most historic speech he would ever witness:

"Soldiers, Sailors, and Airmen of the Allied Expeditionary Force: You are about to embark upon the Great Crusade, toward which we have striven

Lest We Forget

these many months. The eyes of the world are upon you. The hopes and prayers of liberty-loving people everywhere march with you. In company with our brave Allies and brothers-in-arms on other Fronts, you will bring about the destruction of the German war machine, the elimination of Nazi tyranny over the oppressed peoples of Europe, and security for ourselves in a free world.

"Your task will not be an easy one. Your enemy is well trained, well equipped and battle hardened. He will fight savagely.

"But this is the year 1944! Much has happened since the Nazi triumphs of 1940-41. The United Nations have inflicted upon the Germans great defeats, in open battle, man-to-man. Our air offensive has seriously reduced their strength in the air and their capacity to wage war on the ground. Our Home Fronts have given us an overwhelming superiority in weapons and munitions of war, and placed at our disposal great reserves of trained fighting men. The tide has turned! The free men of the world are marching together to Victory!

"I have full confidence in your courage and devotion to duty and skill in battle. We will accept nothing less than full Victory!"

The Beginning of the End of WWII?

AIRBORNE EQUIPMENT 5 JUNE 1944

1) World War 2 manufactured MI910 pattern canteen cover.
2) M1942 aluminum canteen, and m1942 pattern cup with hooks to ALLOW allow fixing to belt.
3) Map pouch for escape and evasion: this contained a map of Normandy coastline, a compass and a small saw blade.
4) M 193 6 'musette' field bag.
5) Cigarettes, Zippo lighter; ration packs, soap, laces, shaving brush, razor, comb, toothbrush and tooth paste, bath towel and handkerchief
6) French currency.
7) 1943 identification ('dog') tags and chain.
8) Wrist-worn compass, with leather strap
9) Spoon.
10) First pattern parachutist's rope coil (c. 33ft J10.05m long).
11) Mk-II A 1 fragmentation grenade
12) Cricket: the 'double-click' sound was used for attracting the attention of fellow airborne troops at night or in poor visibility.
13) M1A1 Thompson sub-machine gun, with 30-round magazine below.
14) A 20-round Thompson magazine pouch.
15) Carton of .45 ammo, and single round.
16) 3x30-round and 5x20-round .45 magazine pouches.
17) 30-round .45 magazine bag with strap (carries up to 8 magazines).
18) M15 White phosphorous smoke grenade (often employed as an anti personnel grenade).
19) M18 colored smoke grenade.
20) Survival kit, containing food, fire lighters, and other basic survival items.
21) First-aid pouch, containing a dressing and morphine.
22) Morphine solution and syrette. 23 Field dressing, and tourniquet.
24) MS black gas mask, M7 black rubberized canvas carrying bag.
25) M3 trench knife and M6 scabbard: usually this was attached to the lower leg.
26) MI910 entrenching tool and cloth cover.
27) B4 ('Mae West') life preserver.
28) 101st Airborne Division shoulder patch.

This depiction is of the uniform and equipment of the 101st Airborne Division. Compiled by Bob Andrade, Courtesy of the Palm Springs WWII Museum.

Lest We Forget

General Maxwell Taylor stepped forward with a command that was different this time. It was urgent, "Get in there and fight, Big Team."

As ammunition was being issued, the mess hall was being prepared for the finest available steak or chicken dinner, and Russ's favorite dessert, ice cream. Russ described the memory, "One night we were having ice cream, the next we were in the middle of battle."

Russ went on to describe how much that ice cream meant to him. Ice cream's not to die for. It's to live for. He would hold onto that thought and look forward to a big bowl of double chocolate ice cream – after the war.

Spring had sprung. England is the most beautiful in June. After a cold winter freeze, the men began to thaw and enjoy the beauty of fresh flowers and feminine, familiar faces that a war could not keep from blooming. Instead, the men were brought together for instructions, details, maps, specifics on sand-tables, all of the scoop that included overwhelming, mind-boggling information. DIRECTIONS: Secure the Beach Exits, Protect 7th Corps south flank, siege bridges, cut cables; 4th Division at H hour to Utah Beach.

Col. Sink stood by the Battle Maps, as he looked and spoke directly to his men. He requested from the Air Corps, "Just get us where we're suppose to go and we'll do the rest." The paratroopers were promised relief in three days.

The Beginning of the End of WWII?

"During every practice jump and dry run there was another guy who checked our parachute to be sure we were hooked up right," Russ recalled. "At first, rolling our parachute was done by the instructors before hours and hours of practice doing it over and over until we knew beyond any doubt that it was done exactly right. If it wasn't and it didn't work, the rip cords wouldn't open the chute or the static line wouldn't when jumping from the C-47. Our life was in our own hands because during battle all the parachutes would be thrown in a pile and we would grab one to strap on before entering the C-47. We wouldn't know who packed it. We had learned to trust and respect each other. I trusted the others as much as I trusted myself. We knew that night there would be no one else to blame if we fell to our death, because our Currahee theme was, 'We stand alone, together.'"

Lest We Forget

F. Russell Snell, shown seated in scooped-out C-47 bucket seat approximately where he sat on D-Day. He stood, looked up at the static line where the paratroopers hooked up their parachute, and then stood in the doorway of the airplane much like he would have, June 6, 1944. (Courtesy Palm Springs WWII Air Museum, 2013.)

The Beginning of the End of WWII?

When the Palm Springs WWII Air Museum acquired a vintage C-47 airplane, Russ wanted to take me aboard to show what the plane looked like on the inside. We climbed the steep stairs and stepped through the massive door. Leaning forward to keep our balance while walking up the steep slope, we worked our way towards the cockpit. Russ pointed out remarkable details on the plane as though his jump was yesterday. He described how he slung the packed chute around his shoulders. The 60-120 pound weight of the packs depended on the size of the man and shape of what they carried. What some of them carried, weighed more than they did. What they packed was so familiar that they each knew what was in the fold of each pocket and in every space of their bag. Paratroopers knew where everything was so that they could reach for anything at any given moment, inside or outside of their uniform. Russ pointed at the static line and showed me how they hooked up.

While loading the planes for the Normandy invasion, everyone expected the routine inspection to ensure their safety, but for some reason it seemed more difficult this time. Maybe it was that steak dinner and ice cream, earlier that night! While checking and assisting each other to be sure everything was done correctly, there was a lot of yelling going on: "'Come on. Pull your gut in.' 'I am. It fit fine last time.' 'Give me a hand over here.' 'I can't believe it's taking you so long.'"

Lest We Forget

General Eisenhower was walking among his men to wave them on, personally speaking to paint-faced men with camouflaged helmets, fighting boots, and their brim-full pockets on the Army tan uniforms. The men remembered what Eisenhower had said and now they experienced his personal individual interest in the men as another message of support was read to them from Field Marshall B. L. Montgomery:

> The time has come to deal the enemy a terrific blow in Western Europe. The blow will be struck by the combined sea, land, and air forces of the Allies-together constituting one great Allied team, under the supreme command of General Eisenhower.
>
> On the eve of this great adventure I send my best wishes to every soldier in the Allied team. To us is given the honor of striking a blow for freedom which will live in history; and in the better days that lie ahead, men will speak with pride of our doings. We have a great and a righteous cause.
>
> Let us pray that 'The Lord Almighty in Battle' will go forth with our armies, and that His special providence will aid us in the struggle.

The Beginning of the End of WWII?

I want every soldier to know that I have complete confidence in the successful outcome of the operations that we are now about to begin. With stout hearts, and with enthusiasm for the contest, let us go forward to victory.

And, as we enter the battle, let us recall the words of a famous soldier spoken many years ago:

> He either fears his fate too much,
> Or his deserts are small,
> Who dare not put it to the touch,
> To win or lose it all.

There was confidence built in the values of the men, knowing their family, home town, and nation were united behind them. Strong leadership gave them courage and strength with a fearless respect in "The Lord Almighty." There was no discomfort or embarrassment being seen in prayer or in talking about God. Many of the troops knew that a Churchill adviser had organized a group who dropped whatever they were doing at designated hours to pray. For one minute they collectively prayed for England, the safety of its people, and that the battle would bring back peace and security.

It took hours to load and nearly four hours flight into Normandy. To some it seemed like they

Lest We Forget

always got to the back of the line, because everyone wanted to get going and get it done. During the dark cover of night, with the troops, supplies and equipment all in place, the 101st, 506 Airborne began flying across the English Channel. The deafening roar of engines pulled into a cloud-covered night sky formation. Like a multitude of hidden, scattered stars, each plane carried strong muscular groups of 24 to 28 men per plane. Row upon row of airships, including many with gliders, headed for the Invasion. No practice run or demonstration this time because as far as America was concerned, the war had just begun, but it would soon become the end of the beginning of WWII.

13
Crossing the English Channel
— Russ is Anxious to Jump

"Destiny is not a matter of chance, it is a matter of choice; it is not a thing to be waited for, it is a thing to be achieved."
— William Jennings Bryant

The paratroopers were in deep thought while flying the 100 miles across the English Channel. There was nothing else they could have done to be better prepared. It was second nature for these professionals to perform under every circumstance, whether it was how to roll their chutes or how to roll when their bodies hit the ground.

How to roll was still second nature when Russ was 87 years old! He came back from playing golf one day and had a surface skinned elbow. I asked, "What happened to you?"

He laughed and said, "Well, I was riding with John. He went up a hill pretty fast, turned sharply, and it threw me out of his golf cart. Seems like everyone saw me and they kept asking, 'Are you OK?' I just had to say, 'I'm a paratrooper. I know how to roll.'"

The heavily weighed down troops could hardly move enough in the darkness of the crowded, cramped flight to view some flickering lights in a few homes along the English coastline.

Lest We Forget

So this was D-Day, June 6, 1944, and their jump to destiny had begun. A special war correspondent, Ward Smith, sat in one of the planes and wondered if the date of the invasion had been leaked, but decided it wouldn't matter if it had because of the force and numbers that were about to land. Smith described some of the events on the plane when someone started to sing, but it was muffled by the loud roar of the engines. The faded-red-light made the faces of the men turn blue, echoing their sickened, sinking stomachs. Smith said some were in shut-eyed, pensive silence. The lips of others were moving, probably saying a prayer, but Smith thought the maneuvers were brilliant.

What do you think about when the mission is to save lives, knowing you had a big chance of losing your own? Do you think about someone you love, your favorite last meal, something you wish you had said, or written home about? As Russ lips moved, he was repeating his favorite text, Psalms 23, that his mother taught him before she died.

While crossing the English Channel, hundreds of C-47s roared towards the airborne assault, preparing to drop thousands from the sky. The jump would be met by a German counterattack that would make their struggle to survive the flak seem mild in comparison to being ripped to shreds when they landed in the killing zone.

With all the uncomfortable equipment strapped on their back, the hard bucket seats

Crossing the English Channel

crowded tightly against them. Anxiously, when hearing the crash of metal, the paratroopers hearts beat faster. Everyone was ready to jump as the huge airships neared the Normandy coastline and the flak started to explode and hit the planes. The pilots were prepared and expected to be attacked as soon as seen. They started to zigzag through the sky while lowering for the jumps. The plan was detailed and everyone knew their exact assignment.

It was impossible to get all of the C-47 planes in their assigned location at the same time. As each phase advanced, the German forces knew the invasion had begun and the Nazi army retaliated with their own well-prepared force. The attack was so intense that the 101st forces feared for their life before even making it to the ground. It seemed safer anywhere than in the plane. Russ just wanted out and said, "All of us thought we had a better chance being a smaller target in a parachute than in the plane."

Flak hit and burst into metal shrapnel of chaos, destruction, crashing planes, injuries and death. It was huge hail-like pounding against the plane, right through a wing or into the sides, creating gaping holes that sent some airships as fiery, fierce, fuel flame meteors to the ground. The flak was followed with tracers of rainbow arches of color that if on the 4th of July would have been beautiful, creating great oohs and ahs! But there was no beauty in this display. Flak was a good

Lest We Forget

reason to get out of the plane. The men were in silent shock, waiting anxiously for their turn to jump out into the treacherous dark night.

A bright red, four minute light appeared and the men on Russ's plane knew their turn had arrived to jump into the depth of darkness and escape the inside whale-shaped belly of the massive C-47 before it exploded. "When the green light flashed," Russ added, "It meant to follow the commands: 'Stand Up. Hook Up. Sound off. Equipment check. Close up. At the door. Jump.'"

Shortly after midnight the jumps began. Russ turn was around 2:00 A.M., when most people would have been getting their soundest sleep. Instinctively the paratroopers clutched the outside of the door, not the inside of the airplane, knowing there was no chance or opportunity to hold on, resist, or refuse to jump. In that position they could push out with more strength.

I asked, "Is it correct that during the jump men were given a war cry word to yell? When you jumped were you told to yell 'Geronimo' or something?"

"Yes, we were told to scream 'Currahee.'"

"What did you say?"

"Get the hell out of here!"

Russ descriptively explained, "If anyone was afraid to jump on that day, they would have pushed us out. We knew that the equipment on our back was just as important as we were. We had to jump!

Crossing the English Channel

But we wanted to jump and get out of that plane before it exploded.

"We knew how to do it, how the jerk on the static line felt to open the chute and how it felt to free-fall through the air, but we were hardly given enough room for the chute to open. The planes were flying too low, about 500 feet, even 250 feet from the ground, so it just took a few swishes in the air and we were rolling on the ground."

The planes were in such danger of being struck that they were going much too fast. The speed and low altitude hurled and propelled the men to the ground so hard that many were badly bruised for over a week and some received broken legs and arms during the jump. It was the worst jump in their career, but it was under the worst conditions. God only knows what each man experienced. Every pilot and paratrooper had a unique memory and story to tell. Perhaps they landed amidst a field of weapons being fired at them, perhaps in water, a tree, a church steeple. Some would die without a chance to ever tell their story, others never would or could. For many, the story from that day on would only be shared between them and their God. There were stories that are kept in silence or buried with the men of the 101st.

Many critics speak of the mistakes made by pilots dropping the paratroopers in the wrong location on D-Day. It's easy to react after the facts,

Lest We Forget

without considering that the invasion was complicated by changing weather, low cloud cover, the amount of flak, tracers, and strength of the enemy. Looking at Russ's life as a paratrooper and having him share his memories, he never attempted to question the actions of the commanding officers or "Conductor Generals," because the circumstances of war require adaptation, quick, untried decisions and risks. There was not a single man who did less than his very best.

The reason Russ never talked about the war for so many years was as he always put it, "I'm no hero. I just did what I had to do at the time. Why me? Why did I live and others die?" He always got teary-eyed when he said, "The heroes are the ones who gave their life, the ultimate sacrifice. They're the heroes. They sacrificed it all."

The 506 could tell thousands of stories and Russ thought the stories of others were more important. He said, "I was just a Pfc.," but knowing some of his officers I knew the value for every one of the men, like their motto said, to stand alone, together as one.

"Honey," attempting to be reassuring, "I need to tell you something. As a registered nurse, I felt about the nurses aides and cleaning staff, that without them, nothing would have run right. Think about what Eisenhower and Churchill said to the 101st and there should be no doubt in your mind any longer that each of you are extraordinary. Lest

Crossing the English Channel

we forget, that's why it's important to tell your story."

The prop blast current, speed of the plane, and impact of the forceful jump is what gave some paratroopers broken legs. Valuable supplies were lost when their leg bags broke off and as much as they tried, some were never found. Russ's leg bag held secure and he suffered no injuries other than scrapes and bruises during the jump. His plane arrived as planned and he jumped in the right location.

Once on the ground, the paratroopers instinctively unhooked the parachute, or grabbed their Army knife to cut loose the rope web, tangled around the chute. The next priority was to stay alive. Russ is a quiet, sentimental person, whose humility is a great strength of being an exemplary, courageous soldier. His judgment is still shown with few words, but strong convictions and values. That is how Russ has always told his own story. He took a moment to grab his Army knife and cut a big round circle hole through his parachute and stick it in his pocket. "I was going to have something to take back home." Russ paused as he pulled out a larger piece of his parachute from his briefcase. He got teary-eyed whenever he showed it. Emotionally he paused a moment, "It's something I could give to my family someday, my good luck charm, and symbol of thankfulness to God for sparing my life."

Lest We Forget

The parachutes were left abandoned, never to be used again, but someone may have found Russ's parachute and wondered how that particular one got such a big hole taken from its side. After a safe drop and roll from the C-47, that jagged cut out piece of Russ's camouflaged silk parachute was stuffed into a secure corner of a pocket. He reached for his toy cricket, knowing the next most important thing was to find the others from his company. He was vulnerable, amidst the strength and forces of the enemy. He was in Normandy.

V.
SCREAMING EAGLE BATTLES AND CHALLENGES

"The eyes of the world are upon you... I have full confidence in your devotion to duty and skill in battle."

-General Dwight D. Eisenhower,
Supreme Allied Commander

14
Normandy, D-Day, June 6, 1944
— Russ's Destiny

"To really live, one must almost die."

— *Unknown*

Heavily loaded down and anxious as all the paratroopers were to get started, Russ was actually fortunate to not jump into the dark, dreary night until 2:00 A.M. He emphasized, "When we landed behind the lines in Normandy we were to find the others from our Company by making one click, 'click-clack' on a toy cricket. Then if someone heard us, they were to answer back with two clicks, 'click-clack, click-clack.'"

When some paratroopers landed, it did not take them very long to realize they were in the wrong location. That unplanned complication made it so much more difficult to reunite with their own unit. Russ landed where he was supposed to be and was not stranded for very long. He still met up unexpectedly with men from the 506, 2nd Battalion, Easy Company, as well as with the 505 and 502 of the 82nd Airborne.

"While trying to reunite with my group, word spread quickly not to use the toy cricket because the Nazi Germans had figured out our signal. When the enemy started answering with the toy taken off of dead American bodies, some of the 101st

Lest We Forget

answered back and it led to their death. Thinking they were answering to a fellow paratrooper, it was letting the enemy know our location." Russ's voice trembled. He shook his head and paused, "A terrible way to get killed."

The picturesque hedgerows of France were beautiful to look at, but were unexpected traps. The enemy waited like gangsters to attack from their hideouts, taking the troopers by surprise and many to their death. The rest of the night and throughout the day, continued with heavy fighting until the 506, Company C gradually met up with others from their unit. Following their intense training to fight, defend, and advance alongside ad hoc units, Charlie Company needed to find the rest of their group in order to secure the French town they were assigned. It was not that they were doing it alone, but each Company had their own assignment. After leaving the blitz-bombed, blasted, devastated English countryside, the Americans became bleeding, battered paratroopers in Normandy.

St. Marie-du-Mont was much like other quaint little villages across the Northwestern coast of France on the beautiful Cotentin Peninsula. Another similarity to other towns was that each seemed to have a picturesque historic 800-1000 year old church with a familiar tall, pictorial steeple. The Germans could hide there and see clear across the French countryside to Normandy's coast, five to six miles away. When the Nazi officer

Normandy, D-Day, June 6, 1944

and battalion saw hundreds of landing craft coming ashore with more warships than they knew we had, some of the forces were pulled out from St. Marie-du-Mont to defend Normandy's Utah Beach. The paratroopers caught the enemy by surprise, landing behind the enemy lines from St. Marie-du-Mont, clear to Cherborg. The Paratroopers mission kept them focused on securing their objective to free the town they were assigned and to continue the advancement.

The Nazi Col. Von der Heydte roared back, sending stronger forces to defend and secure the town against the combined efforts of the various paratrooper units. Airborne were already there fighting in what would become the unmerciful, unending, tenacious and tough battle of St. Marie-du-Mont because the enemy was on both sides of them, almost like another hole in the doughnut.

I hesitated to ask, but I wondered if all of the paratroopers carried grenades. In answer to my question, Russ really hesitated but replied, "Each of us must have carried two or three grenades in our bag." I could tell he didn't want to talk about it. With that much destructive power in his own hand, why would he want to tell us and talk about it?

Screaming Eagles were falling and dying as they were being shot at from every direction, all around and beside Russ. They were surrounded with the sounds of machine guns, bullets, and grenades, but when hearing the cry, "Medic. Here,

Lest We Forget

over here. I need you," that was the loudest sound of all. Without realizing it, Russ experienced the beginning of hearing loss in both ears as the result of battle and the emotional sound that would cause permanent post traumatic stress.

Finally, one man was able to reach for his grenade, accurately threw and landed it on his target, blowing off the church steeple where the firing was coming from. It ended some of the brutal killing of so many of their own. The 506 and other troopers partnering together were the first to secure a French Town, the town closest to Utah Beach and Russ was part of that battle.

The Nazi flag was taken down, but the American flag was not raised by Company C as planned. Joe Reed had a U. S. flag tucked under his parachute harness intending to plant it firmly in the ground, but his T-5 chute failed. He had to be released and quickly left his chute and flag behind. The paratroopers were not there to occupy, but restore freedom to the people of France, who cheered when they saw an American flag raised.

The Normandy invasion defied the fog and flak with tenacity and toughness. The Nazi referred to the paratroopers of the 101st as Yankee butchers with big pockets, but those pockets were filled with the means for what Omar Bradley called, "The Eagle Soldiers who destroyed the myth of German invincibility" and the methodical, meticulous

Normandy, D-Day, June 6, 1944

maneuvers of training would continue to be improved upon during battle.

Success in Normandy depended on successfully overtaking Carentan and the Screaming Eagles were chosen for the assignment that lasted over thirty days without relief. Heavily guarded canals, swamps, and the disadvantage of not knowing the lay of the land struck down the paratroopers repeatedly, but it did not keep them down. If one was fallen, others seemed to acquire twice the strength to carry on, strength they never knew they had, strength beyond their training when they had been pushed beyond human capability. The route to Carentan became known as "Purple Heart Lane."

The Currahee men on the ground had it rougher than anyone else, but they were tougher than anyone else. The troop Carrier Groups, B-17 bomber, air Corp, and C-47 Pilots lives were in danger of being blown up on every mission, but like a B-17 pilot friend, neighbor, and golf partner, Wayne Stump, said to us, "We could at least get back to an airport or headquarters most of the time for a decent, not always good, but decent hot meal and secure place to sleep."

Wayne continued, "When I was a B-17 pilot, I could find the instruments blindfolded." He was a hero pilot of a record 29 combat and six humanitarian missions for a total of 35, when only 25 were required. As a 569th Bomb Squadron pilot, his

Lest We Forget

"Shady Lady" crew never received a scratch, but their plane was heavily damaged, and full of flak holes on repeated occasions. During flight they dropped chaff aluminum to jam the German radar. He said, "When a higher bomber drop went between my No. 3 engine and left side of the fuselage, I could see the paint on the bomb." On London evenings that some claimed felt safe and secure, Wayne recalled, "I could see and hear V1 buzz bombs headed our way."

Another of Russ's friends, like all of the WWII Greatest Generation Veterans, was a quiet humble man, John Santucci, owner of their family Capri Restaurant, Desert Hot Springs, California. When many went there to eat because of the excellent Italian food, few knew the background of his WWII experience in the Philippines. John was hit by an anti-aircraft weapon that nearly tore off his arm and he was taken in a semi-conscious state to an improvised church hospital. He was placed in the ward with other men of less priority because they were not expected to live.

Days later, a doctor ordered an X-ray and found that the unexploded shell was still in John's arm. The risk was too high, but the brave military doctor took the chance and cautiously, successfully removed the shell. John Santucci remained in the Hospital for several years and suffered the effects of his wounds for the rest of his life but he had miraculously survived and had a story so

Normandy, D-Day, June 6, 1944

astounding that it was told in Ripley's "Believe It Or Not."

On the ground, paratroopers had rations for meals and no sleeping bag or improvised shower. They just kept "going and going and going," with recharged batteries of determination, will power, and courage. They tried to grab a few winks of sleep, whether "dug in" to fox holes or from bunkers, behind the rubble of war, or wherever they could stop fighting long enough as a group. If they did, the sounds and images of battle were still on their minds.

The goal of 101st Airborne was never trying to over-shadow, get the glory, attempt to outshine or impress their officers and other men. It was a joint effort. Young paratroopers thought they were bigger than life, but they certainly didn't think they were better. They knew all along that many would die during the fight, but every paratrooper didn't believe it would happen to him. The 506, Company C had fought together for the freedom of St. Marie-du-Mont. While advancing to Carentan amidst machine gun fire, 105mm cannon dug underground, hidden behind hedgerows of rubble and dead buddies around him, Russ received a gunshot wound to his right arm, June 13, 1944. Russ went down with his first injury, after eight days of intense, continuous battle on Purple Heart Lane. His focus was to get back up and keep

Lest We Forget

fighting with his Band of Brothers who were there to help him.

The other heroes were the medics who risked their lives to rescue the injured. Russ's "good" arm was his right arm that was hit and made it impossible to keep fighting or defending for very long. He was weakened from loss of blood, taken out, and transported to a hospital in London for treatment, but even now, there was good news. Russ was alive.

15
Normandy Nurse
— Marjorie Imagines Being a WWII Nurse

"No act of kindness, no matter how small, is ever wasted."

— Aesop

While Russ was fighting a real war, I was playing war back home in Amarillo, Texas. In my little white pinafore play dress uniform as a nurse, I pretended to be a real nurse. My brother Trevor and little neighbor boy were fighting and I was ready to go in and take care of their wounds when they got shot. We were pretending, from what we heard around us, to be fighting just like we were in the Army. Kids used to play Cowboys and Indians, but Trevor and our little friend had toy helmets, play guns and sticks for weapons. During WWII children started to fight a different kind of war.

I was also pretending to be a nurse, when I imagined caring for Russ following the Normandy wounds, qualifying him for a Purple Heart.

WWII NURSE IN NORMANDY

I felt a weak pat on my arm. Turning, I looked into Russ's compas-sionate eyes expressing appre-ciation for the care nurses were giving under

Lest We Forget

the most difficult conditions. Determining who could be saved and who needed help the most, as I rushed around and was close enough, Russ reached out and touched me before I could approach him. Showing he had been watching and appreciated what nurses were doing for others, he touched me.

Russ's body was terribly weak, unbelievably tired and shaken. Through his war-painted face, I could still see how pale he was getting, on the verge of unconsciousness. His uniform was stiffened from dry blood and his war-battled body was covered with layers of dirt, hardened against his body, but he was able to show compassion for my battle against death to save the living. My nursing creed was pledging before God to aid the physician in his duty and devote myself to the welfare of those committed to my care. "Political correctness" would later remove the word God and overlook the strength that faith in God gave America during World War II.

The men were starving and dehydrated, in need of a good bath, fluids, and most of all, sleep. The nurses and doctors were a team,

Normandy Nurse

organized and doing the best we possibly could with so many injured arriving continuously. Pressure dressings had been applied and the bleeding had for the most part been stopped. The doctors had been giving orders from every corner of the room: sutures, stitches, scissors, bandage, wound care, arm splint, leg brace, water, fluids. The nurses were following orders and sometimes doing things without an order.

As soon as possible I went back to Russ who was finally assigned a room that was crowded with other paratroopers. As he collapsed into his own bed, he could actually look out the window with a view of the battlefield. He was relieved to be in the care of his Angels of Mercy. As he settled into his bed, bathed, and given clean hospital clothing, he asked me if I would check his pocket to see if a piece of his parachute was there. I picked up the bag and told him with reassurance, that yes it was and I put it in a pocket of his clean, new uniform. Now, get some sleep, I told him.

Russ's recovery was rapid once he was transferred to a hospital in England. I was fortunate to accompany many of the injured. As his

Lest We Forget

energy and strength returned, I knew Russ's arm wound would soon be healed sufficiently to be discharged back to his group. I also knew that emotional scars can take longer to heal than physical wounds and so I asked Russ why I had not seen him writing any letters back home and to the best of my knowledge, he hadn't received any either. I asked if there was a reason for that, because others were writing home every day.

After hearing Russ's reply, I told him that I felt he should write home anyway. I felt that I knew him well enough to believe he was dearly loved by his family and friends. I told him whatever he decided was alright, but if he would like to, he could write to me. I promised that I would answer and imagined handing him a note with my contact number address as a Military Nurse. Everyone needs to know that someone is thinking about them. That's the true meaning of TLC.

16
A Purple Heart Recovery
— Russ is "Fine and Dandy"

*"Scars heal. Glory fades.
All we're left with are memories made."*
— *Chris Cagel*

Russ has an amazing inner strength. He didn't feel that he had anyone to write home to while recovering, because his dad had been moving him around to other family members since he was nine years old when his mother died. His dad, Thomas, had recently remarried and was busy with a new family. Russ's sister Alice was not living and his brother Tom had been drafted into the Army shortly after getting married. It seemed natural to assume that all of Russ's best friends were probably in the service as well.

It was important for Russ to be self-sufficient and not be a burden to anyone any longer. He didn't even want his high school sweetheart Rosemary to worry about him in case he was killed during battle. Russ thought it would cause less pain and be easier to go on with her life if he broke up with her before enlisting and entering paratrooper training.

"After giving it a lot of thought," Russ explained to me, "I decided the best way to do it was to make her mad at me."

Lest We Forget

Since I never knew Rosemary, I wondered why Russ decided to do that because many young men proposed to their girl friends and wanted to get married before they went off to war. Rosemary was a red head and might have had the unfair assumption or reputation of getting angry easily. I thought Russ might be taking advantage of that temperament if it was true in her case!

Russ described what he did. "I went to the home of another girl in our school and explained to her my situation, concern, and decision. I told her, 'If I can make Rosemary jealous and angry at me, she might be glad I'm going off to paratrooper training. She won't have to see me around here anymore or think about me when I'm gone off to war and she can date someone else.'

"I borrowed my brother's car, picked Ellen up and we drove back and forth in front of Rosemary's home. I honked the horn on Tom's 1937 Chevy Sedan until Rosemary finally came out into the yard to see what was going on. Maybe that was a little mean of me to be seen with someone else, but it worked. Now I knew she wouldn't be home worried or crying about me going off to war. She could go on with her life without mourning the loss of mine, because I knew I might not come back."

While others were writing home every day, Russ thought if he had no one to write home to, it would be easier on him not to expect an answer. What a remarkable, unselfish thing to do. I want to

A Purple Heart Recovery

believe that if I was Russ's girl friend I would have figured him out or I would have said to him, "You're not going to get away with that. If you don't want me, I don't have to be your girlfriend anymore, but I want to... no, I will write you so tell me right now how to do that. If you won't tell me, I'll get your military address from your dad or brother Tom. You can depend on me to write, because I love you."

As much as I'd like to think that's what I would have done, I realize that as a young person I may not have been able to stand up so courageously to a "boyfriend" who was going off to war as a man. With the mind of a mature person, I honestly think that would have been the right thing to do.

Recalling when I was a young teenager, when our family moved from Georgetown, British Guiana to Kingston, Jamaica, 1953, I received a letter from my first boy friend, Kenneth. Embarrassed that my parents would want to read his letter, I decided to discard the letter and not answer him. The second and third time he wrote I did the same thing until Kenneth quit writing. Years later I was aware how inconsiderate that was. I treated him rudely by not answering his letters and explaining that we were too far separated by thousands of miles to write and keep in touch.

On June 22, 1944, Russ did decide to write a note on the back of the "Restricted Memo from Headquarters 62 D, General Hospital APO 350, U. S.

Lest We Forget

Army." The government postcard notified Russ's dad, "Your son Francis R. Snell was awarded the Purple Heart for wounds received in action 13 Jun 44 in France, European Theater of Operations."

At the top of the military postcard, Russ wrote a short note in his wonderful strong penmanship, "I'm fine and dandy so please don't worry. I got out of the hospital a few days ago. Write to me at my old address now, Co. C. 506 P.I.R." Russ had come as close to death as the flak pounding against his C-47, the bomb blast from an 88, the barrel of a gun, and that was enough to decide to ask if someone from back home would write him a letter.

I love Russ for his positive attitude. Using the phrase to his dad, "I'm fine and dandy," after all he had just gone through during the Normandy Invasion, shows you can't keep a good man down. The original "Yankee Doodle Boy" song had just been rewritten by George Cohan for a Broadway Musical. "Little Johnny Jones," was first performed in 1942 by James Cagney, but during war, the patriotic words and melody became popular among the military: "I'm a Yankee Doodle Dandy, A Yankee Doodle, do or die, A real live nephew of my Uncle Sam, Born on the Fourth of July."

Instead of being the Yankee Doodle Dandy going to town on a pony, Russ was the Yankee Doodle paratrooper about to board the C-47 going to the town of Zon, Holland for another parachute

A Purple Heart Recovery

jump. He was "fine and dandy" and had a job to "do or die."

17
Zon, Holland, The Market Garden, Sunday Punch, September 17, 1944
— Russ's Oak Leaf Cluster

"Better to die fighting for freedom than to be a prisoner all the days of your life."

— Bob Marley

Family reunions are centered around great food. We had taken time to enjoy what everyone brought of Russ's favorites: Lisa's famous cheese ball, Tanya's delicious fresh salsa as well as guacamole, and Brittany's stuffed mushrooms for appetizers. Rick grilled his delicious Spinach-Arugula burgers while Rob masterfully grilled corn on the cob and skewers. Jane made her traditional pea salad, and Natalie brought her favorite, the "world's best macaroni salad." Tyler made the buck-eye candy that Michael started calling "one-eyed dog bites" when he was three years old!

After our big meal, Russ went back to his comfortable rocking chair on the porch. He was carrying a big bowl of Missy's cake size slice of triple chocolate chip brownie, drizzled with hot fudge syrup and fresh garden-ripened strawberries piled on top of the rich vanilla ice cream.

I laughed, "All that good food and you still eat to be polite, so you can get to the dessert!"

Lest We Forget

The entire morning had been spent visiting and asking Russ questions about the war. We didn't want to rush him while eating, but after his last bite of that no-calorie dessert, I brought attention back to the discussion, "What was it like going back to your unit after being injured and in the hospital?"

"There were so many replacements that I hardly recognized my own group, but it gave heart to those who remained and hope we could carry on... that their lost lives would not be in vain," Russ paused and answered sadly.

While the 101st spent a whole year in England waiting for invasion orders, the officers and Command Staff at Camp Toccoa, Fort Benning, Camp Mackall and Fort Bragg had sufficient time to continue preparing and training more 101st Airborne who became the replacements. In Normandy, the 101st, 506 suffered the loss of 233 men who were killed in action. Another 26 were missing in action. Russ continued to explain to us, "We had no idea what was happening all around us, because we just knew what had to be done in our own small area."

It's a good thing that the 101st Airborne didn't know. Twelve thousand Allied Forces had died during the two months preceding D-Day. Today in Germany, there are eighty thousand graves still tended after the loss of their own troops, a constant reminder of WWII. Historians say that construction

Zon, Holland, The Market Garden, Sunday Punch, September 17, 1944

work still unearths the skeletons of soldiers who died and an accurate, definitive death toll may never be known. The best estimate is that the total of Allied and German troops killed, wounded and missing is 425,000. Of that number 200,000 German troops were killed or wounded, and 83,000 from the 21st Soldier Group of England, Canadian and Polish forces died before the Americans came to help end the war. There were 19,000 innocent civilians who lost their lives before the Americans were involved. The U. S. Army Center of Military History estimates that the United States lost 6,035 and another 5,000 Allied force heroes. These are startling, shocking statistics that apply to the Normandy invasion alone.

Russ and I had talked about post-war feelings and why these facts are important to his story. Most Germans today condemn what happened. Some still feel outraged, but forgiven and accept that they have no guilt. Germans today should not feel they have to keep saying they are sorry, but some still feel ashamed. There are those who cannot believe the war was as bad as reported, but it's shocking that in today's world there are those who still believe in the Nazi cause or deny the holocaust ever occurred. Telling the facts and feelings about the war, personalizes the human story of brave, courageous, very young men in their late teens and early twenties. Courage is the act of

Lest We Forget

being the only one who knows you're scared to death.

Before Russ's jump into Zon, Holland, the troops knew exactly what to expect as they boarded the huge, thundering C-47s. It was called The Second D-Day, but became known as the Sunday Punch. The 506 knew they could do it. They had done it before and knew they would be successful again, but there was a difference. It was even worse than in Normandy.

When discharged from the London Hospital after the bullet wound to his right arm, Russ found the inner strength needed to carry on from Eisenhower's description that "caution and timidity is not the same thing." Russ had the caution to be alert to circumstances, knowing he would again be surrounded with blood-shed. He prayed to get his full courage back and found the renewed energy and resolve needed to help get this over with and stay alive.

After a brief time to recover, Russ was reunited with his unit in preparation for the next battle. Rest and relaxation, good food, and time spent listening to some good music in the military canteen did little to heal the anguish of what they had already seen and experienced. Words could never describe it. War movies capture emotions, but unless you were there it's impossible to know how it felt.

Zon, Holland, The Market Garden, Sunday Punch, September 17, 1944

Perceived as "cocky paratrooper warriors," there was nothing arrogant or over-confident now that they had experience under their belts. These men became combat veterans who had demonstrated extraordinary heroism. Their outstanding performance in Normandy had already earned the troopers purple hearts, bronze stars and a presidential citation. They had renewed confidence in their mission with hope and prayers that the war would end in the Netherlands.

Being defeated in the Normandy D-Day Invasion, the Nazi Army strategically moved full forces into the Netherlands. They knew the Americans had to be defeated in Holland and prepared for them by demolishing the bridges. The paratroopers knew it meant heavy fighting was awaiting.

After the Nazi bombing and battle of Roterdam, where the highest population of Jewish citizens lived, 75% of them had been killed and those who remained were being sent to concentration camps. Since May, 1940, the Dutch government leaders and royal family were exiled to London when the country was overtaken by the Nazi German occupation.

Russ groaned, "This time the invasion was during the day... about one, two o'clock in the afternoon instead of 2:00 A.M.. We had a reassuring sense that daylight would make it easier because

Lest We Forget

bombers had gone ahead of us to pave the way. We had a sudden, rude awakening."

There was a long pause. The family knew that war stories were not easy to talk about and so we waited to give Russ a chance to gather his thoughts. It had taken Russ a long time to be able to talk about the war. It would have been easier for him to tell about his war experiences and memories at Company C, Airborne reunions with his Band of Brothers who he had something in common with.

After Russ's long sigh, he continued to tell his family about WWII experiences as a paratrooper in the Netherlands. "It was on my brother Tom's birthday, September 17, 1944, when our orders were to load our packs, pockets, and parachutes for another jump. We knew how and where to put everything, but we were given extra supplies, weapons, and ammunition to find a place for."

As the engines coughed and warmed up to a loud bellow, Sargent Snelling checked Russ's parachute and pack straps. The airship rumbled into a deafening roar around Russ as he awkwardly climbed the steps and settled into his bucket seat. Some men were loaded with over 200 pounds including the extra demolitions. As maneuverable as Houdini, struggling for his freedom while underwater in chains, the paratroopers would be performing on a world stage, attempting for civilizations freedom to be restored. The goal was to end the war in the Netherlands.

Zon, Holland, The Market Garden, Sunday Punch, September 17, 1944

The huge, heavy door locked behind them as the paratroopers settled in for take off. Instead of feeling the C-47 start to move, the men in Russ's plane were startled when the airships massive door suddenly reopened. The trembling, thunderous roar of the powerful C-47 engines were not loud enough to prevent the men from noticing when an officer stepped inside and above the ear-piercing roar, they heard his commanding voice, "Snell, off the plane."

"I got up as quickly as I could with my heavy load and awkwardly waddled back down the steps as I was led toward another plane."

Russ followed the directions without any idea of what he had done or why he was the only one pulled off the plane. The C-47 he was on taxied down the runway for takeoff as Russ marched as quickly as he could with his heavy load and heard the strong voice of the officer, "Your assignment has been changed. You'll be working with them in Headquarters."

In bright sunlight, instead of at night, Russ was flying across the English Channel all over again, but this time he was headed towards Zon, Holland. There was enough time during the tense four hour flight to get instructions following his changed assignment. It proved they had confidence in Russ's courage and ability. He was fast, accurate, agile and able.

"You will be working with us in headquarters as a message-carrier on a military Harley Davidson

Lest We Forget

motorcycle. You will be given directions to take messages between other units with instruction where and who to give information to."

During flight, the feelings all came back, of hearts hammering against their chest, mouths so dry they could not swallow. That lumped stomach knot was more than tight uniform straps, securing the packs on their back.

Russ continued to describe how he recalled that day, "It was a tough flight. I knew what to expect after Normandy and it was happening all over again. Suddenly for five, maybe ten minutes without stop, there was constant flak exploding over and under us. Then right through the wing of a plane nearby, I saw a C-47 spinning to the ground. That was the trouble with it being daylight. I could see everything through the small windows across from us. I just wanted out. I had a better chance in my parachute than in a big C-47 target because somehow the flak gets through."

"Then the light came on: the red... then the green light flashed. I stood, hooked up and worked my way toward the door... and jumped."

During combat in France, one of the paratroopers found and retrieved a German Army coronet that gave the Company C men the idea of striking up a big band. It relieved the tension of war to spend some free time humorously turning their metal utility bowls, canteens, and helmets into instruments. Major General Chase ordered that

Zon, Holland, The Market Garden, Sunday Punch, September 17, 1944

each paratrooper have a turn at blowing the coronet until they could each get out one strong note. Hilarity followed as the coronet squeaked, squealed, and struggled to find a pleasing resonant sound from someone. Anyone!

One after another as the men started their jump, with flak bursting in air all around them, they yelled, "Currahee." But, as one man jumped he pulled out what was hidden under his arm. Having perfected his skill and taken the Major Generals order seriously, he let out a long, loud, powerful note on the coronet.

Small talk is for sissies, so it's nice when parachuting into battle, one unidentified hunk made a strong statement with a good sense of humor. Just prior to boarding the C-47 for their 2nd jump, Major General Chase spoke words of encouragement and support to the troops, "Stay strong and proud." With a smile he added, "Make this one the musical jump from the sky," and the paratrooper literally did.

We agreed it was sad, rather than funny, but having a paratrooper's sense of humor was still good medicine for Russ seventy years after the war. While leaning back in his recliner and reading from a magazine about the good old days, Russ read out loud: "Marge, here's a paratrooper advertisement, 'For sale. Parachute. Only used once. Never opened.'"

Lest We Forget

The Currahee album for the 101st 506 was printed in Europe immediately after the war. It included two photographs of F. Russell Snell. He is shown at the paratroopers military canteen in London (third man to the right of the man drinking) just before the Netherlands Invasion. Also shown was Sgt. Forest Snelling, tightening Russ's parachute straps prior to boarding the C-47 plane that crashed. Paul K. Devoe is seen walking beside them.

Zon, Holland, The Market Garden, Sunday Punch, September 17, 1944

The Nazi army had just been defeated in Normandy and surrounding towns so they had moved the strength of their forces to Holland. They were ready for the American and Allied forces because they felt they had to defeat them in the Netherlands. Bridges had been blown up and the paratroopers knew heavy fighting was awaiting.

With his feet firmly on the ground, Russ started releasing the straps to unhitch and abandon his parachute while looking for the white smoke assembly area. As the paratroopers were running, they were watching for the place to reunite with their unit and a ditch to jump into if shot at. Securely finding others from the 506, questions and rumors spread. What happened to that missing plane, the one that Master Sgt. Forest Snelling was on?

"Can't be. That was the C-47 I was on when they pulled me off the plane." Russ was shocked when confirmation reports verified, "The very plane I was on was blown up, killing every man, including Snelling. He just checked my chute and straps before take off."

Russ would never forget that name. Not because of the similarity in their last names, (Snelling and Snell), but because Russ was the only one to survive, simply because he was the only one taken off of the plane before it took off. Suddenly the gun shot wound received on the way to Carentan and all the things Russ had seen seemed

Lest We Forget

insignificant to him. Being pulled off of that plane on the way to the Netherlands was a lot more humbling to live through, too large a coincidence to be attributed to chance. As close as Russ and his brother Tom were, it is easy to understand how a birthday would never be worth celebrating if one of them died on the other's birthday.

Stories have been told of lives saved when a piece of shrapnel pinged off a helmet, buckle or mess kit. Others said it was because a bullet or piece of metal bounced off of a flak jacket or pocket New Testament. While visiting the Patton Museum on D-Day, 2014, Russ pointed out a small Military New Testament inside a glass cabinet and commented, "I wonder what happened to the one I had. It had a metal cover and I kept it in a pocket over my heart," but for the rest of Russ's life, he considered 17, his brother Tom's birthday, to be his lucky number and the Normandy cut out piece of parachute, his lucky charm. Russ lived through his second parachute jump, September 17, 1944.

Once the surviving 506 airborne gathered at the designated location for their next combat mission, Russ had the assurance his camouflage remnant piece of soft silk parachute was safely tucked away. It made it through his combat in St. Marie-du-Mont to Carentan and back to a London hospital following his injury and he intended that piece of silk would still be with him when victorious in the Netherlands.

Zon, Holland, The Market Garden, Sunday Punch, September 17, 1944

The 506 would love to have landed peacefully in the colorful land known for multiple shades of tulips, turning windmills, and chocolate flavored breakfasts while listening to the pleasant sounds of friendly people speaking the Dutch language. The landing of thousands of paratroopers covered the countryside full of scattered bridges, and canals. Many pastures were filled with grazing livestock when the paratroopers landed. It was a vivid memory of breaking loose from a parachute to run and rescue men caught in crashed, burning gliders. Paratroopers could never forget the horrifying experience stepping over dead bodies and climbing over livestock corpse as they desperately tried to save lives.

Many of the worst memories were seldom referred to, but difficult to forget. Years after the war the focus was still trying to make sense of it, trying to think of our society positively, and keep believing in the good of people. On one occasion while some of the Company C men were visiting during a reunion, conversations led to memories about the war. Bob Wiatt told a story from Holland, 1944, when he heard loud, strange noises in the dark and the morning light revealed the troubling view of a field of dead cows.

Sensing the emotion of many painful memories that had been told, Jessie Shelman described his trip back to Holland. It was under positive, better conditions when he revisited the

Lest We Forget

area fifty years after the war. He was struck by the restoration of the colorful, peaceful land of tulips and commented, "Same fields, different cows."

Major General Maxwell Taylor of the 506 was depending on the British forces to secure Eindhoven, but they had been brutally attacked, failing to secure the town. The 101st would have to join others to accomplish the goal. Taylor's strong leadership was guided by a well defined mission, giving the paratroopers the focus and motivation to succeed and reach the Eindhoven objective, five miles away.

In Russ's new assignment as message runner, he worked tirelessly with the commanders in 506 headquarters, to quickly deliver messages between the other battalions. Communication was vital.

The only bridge not destroyed across the Wilhelmina Canal on the way to Eindhoven was in Zon. It had to be preserved at all costs. Within 50 yards of reaching the bridge, it was blown 100 feet into the air and rained down large splintering chip fragments and debris on the men. Amidst dangerous combat, they continued to advance. Paratroopers are not only a sky army; among them were engineers and excellent swimmers who crossed the canal while being fired at. Others followed by swimming or made it across in found rowboats.

Zon, Holland, The Market Garden, Sunday Punch, September 17, 1944

The whole mission would not have been successful if the 506 advance team had not taken 50-100 prisoners. Except for two 88 artillery tanks and crew that were firing at them being destroyed within 15 minutes, the resistance was light. Loyal, appreciative Dutch civilians gathered to help by bringing planks and doors to rebuild the bridge. One volunteer brought out and donated his black-market lumber hidden in his garage.

With one intact bridge column for a foundation, the bridge was rebuilt in less than two hours, wide enough for the battalions to make it across single file by midnight and they headed towards Eindhoven. By 12:30 P.M. the following day, September 18, Eindhoven was secured, the first Dutch city to fall and be liberated. Russ was there just as he was to help secure and liberate the first town in Normandy, St. Marie-du-Mont. Once the cheering people of Holland came out showering the troops with hot-chocolate and pastries, the Nazi Army returned with heavy unexpected bombing. The ground shook as the shrapnel tore up the streets and destroyed buildings.

Russ was beside one of the buildings, all alone in the midst of the battle, aiming, firing, shooting against the enemy who had returned in full force. While steadying his M1 against the corner edge of the structure, he heard Sargent Bill Knight yell, "Snell, over here. I need you."

Lest We Forget

That was a time when natural instinct kicked in and they both knew what to do. Russ knew to run like he was being chased by a lion. Those three-mile training runs up and back down Mt. Currahee with a full pack on his back paid off. Russ slung the rifle over his shoulder and tore across the 100 yards towards the other building where Knight had called him from. Instantly the edifice where Russ had been standing was blown up and fell to the ground in a heap of mortar, dust, and rubble.

The slightest hesitation and Russ would have been buried beneath the destroyed building. Bill Knight became his hero and life long friend. Besides both being Indiana Hoosiers, Russ heartfelt admiration for Sargent Bill Knight occurred again, 1994, when Bill decided to share a very touching letter written to his mother, Mrs Anna Knight. The letter was written from Eindhoven, Netherlands, March 26, 1945, but was not allowed to be mailed for six months because all letters were being held for the protection of the citizens as well as the servicemen.

Aged and yellow for 50 years after being sent, the letter was very meaningful and touching to all of the Company C men when Bill Knight read it to them at the reunion. The letter was especially significant to Russ whose own mother died when he was nine years old. How he would have loved to have his mother to write home to, because Russ

Zon, Holland, The Market Garden, Sunday Punch, September 17, 1944

knew she would have been praying for him and the letter told of Bill's love for his mother:

To Mrs. Anna Knight,
1921-7th Avenue.,
Terre Haute, Indiana,
U. S. A.

From F. Rooymans,
Rechtestr. 5,
Eindhoven, Netherlands

Dear Mrs. Knight,

Half a year ago, on the day of our liberation I did a promise to your son. He was the first allied soldier to enter the street in which we live. It will hardly be possible for you to understand what it means to be liberated! I will not try to make it clear to you; it would take a book.

As your boy and his friends were a bit tired after 24 hours of fighting, we invited them and they had a wash and a drink of ours. Asking him if I could do him a pleasure in some way, his immediate answer was: "Write a letter to my mother." But foreign letters were

Lest We Forget

not allowed and since today only post-traffic is open and I take this first opportunity to keep my promise and to God, that the Dutchmen are very proud of your boys and we are sure that the proudest of all must be you, being his mother.

We thank you and your nation so much for all they did to liberate us from the Kraut and every day we pray for your boys that they may come home safe and sane.

With kind regards from home to home

Once the city of Eindhoven was liberated for the second time, after being murderously shattered through the day, the 506 proceeded towards Uden, 22 miles North. On September 23, 1944, the 2nd Battalion was cornered and had to be released. The 506 proceeded along Hell's Highway between Uden and Vechel, suffering the greatest loss of lives in their fiercest battle in Holland. At that time the highway was cut off again and all three battalions returned towards Uden, reopening Hell's Highway, September 25, never to be cut off again. But the most fanatical and strongest enemy focus continued towards Arnhem until October 5, 1944. During that time Russ rode the Army Harley,

Zon, Holland, The Market Garden, Sunday Punch, September 17, 1944

delivering messages between the three battalions. He was in constant danger and in life-threatening conditions without protection much of the time.

The enemy came back to attack again, October 6, 1944, forcing Russ's First Battalion to withdraw. The 506 would not think of allowing an entire Battalion to be lost. They were relieved that night by a glider infantry as the others went back to assist. The First Battalion joined the others and made another strong attack with the Second and Third Battalions to end the Opheusden action, but it left the city a heap of destruction. During the fiercest fighting and heaviest artillery yet received in Holland, Russ was blown off of the Army Harley Davidson by an 88mm explosion on Hell's Highway where many had to be left dead and dying. Russ had again defied death by being rescued and was unable to go on with his Company to Nijmegan.

While turning the pages and looking at Russ's 1945 Currahee Album together, he said, "Wait, turn that page back. That's Master Sargeant Snelling, checking my parachute straps, and that's my friend Devoe." Russ was pointing at the photograph and said, "That's just before we got on the plane together going to Holland. It's a picture of the C-47 that crashed. I would have been on that very plane if they did not pull me off and change my assignment."

With the blunt led on my No. 2 yellow pencil, I jotted down a note on the page: "Russ, Sargeant

Lest We Forget

Snelling and friend Devoe." The name stuck in my mind and several years later I came across the names again. For seventy years Russ carried the tragic memory that everyone died on that crashed airplane. It was the C-47 he was pulled off of to work in headquarters.

Late one night I was reading from the copies of reunion scrapbooks that we asked Company C Clerk Norm Smith to make for us. "Russ, you're not going to believe what I just found out." I started to read to him from the album.

On March 20, 1956, sixteen-year-old Gerrit van Kleef was digging in his father's garden when his shovel hit a hard object. He pushed deeper around the firm mass, figuring it was a large stone, but was shocked to discover it was a skull. The boy ran to his father who directed him to return and bury the skull where he had found it until they notified the police.

The Arnhem District Dutch Police in the Nijmegan area at 0396 Middenweg Opheusden uncovered the full skeleton accompanied by an inscribed tin first aid kit, metal buckle and Army dog tag. It was Russ's friend Paul K. Devoe. Immediately the burgomaster notified the American Embassy that the "mortal remains of an American soldier had been recovered and identified," but the long awaited translated report was not received by the 101st 506, Company C, Commander Al Hassenzahl, until December, 1995.

Zon, Holland, The Market Garden, Sunday Punch, September 17, 1944

A brick memorial was erected by the citizens in honor of the C-47 stick shot down September 17, 1944, during the Market Garden Operation. The names of fourteen C Company paratroopers are listed on the right hand side and on the left, seventeen Dutch civilians who died when the flaming plane crashed into a barn.

Citizens reported seeing paratroopers jumping out of the burning plane all the way to the ground. Paul Devoe survived the crash, found his way back with other paratroopers, but according to the American grave register, he was killed in combat October 6, 1944 and buried by an American soldier at the Opheusden site.

On the 50th Anniversary of D-Day, Al Hassenzahl, Ted Heintz Claude Scoggins, and his son Jeff had made the highly emotional trip to visit the Nijmegan garden home where Devoe's body was found. Sadly their video and camera report was unavailable because a thief had stolen their equipment.

Immediately several people spoke up at the 1994 Reunion when the story was told and they had seen a documentary on PBS with a full narration of the story. It may never be known if it was their stolen and sold property, or was it coincidence?

Russ and I did not know that five from that plane became POW and at the 1995 reunion in Indianapolis, Indiana, we were sitting at the table

Lest We Forget

with one of the POW survivors, Elvin Homan. The others were: Vic Goble, Moses Lopez, Charles Honecker and Gerald Counts.

In a July, 1943 Department training pamphlet to the 506, they were strictly and clearly given instructions that if they were captured to be aware that "most enemy intelligence comes from prisoners." The military was required to only give their "name, grade, and serial number, attempt to destroy all papers, never talk or give fake stories, and never carry any personal information. Be sensible, use your head," and that meant to be strong, courageous, bold and fearless.

Those five men from Company C knew how to survive as a POW. When the war was over they were released, marched for days, and found their way back to the men of their unit. Paul Devoe escaped while being one of the POW, found his way to return to the 506, fought on while suffering with his crash injuries, but was killed in action October 6, 1944. That was the same day Russ was injured. When Devoe died, there was at least one paratrooper who risked his life to stay and bury him in an unmarked garden grave. While digging a grave for one of their own, it was done with love, mercy, a prayer and belief that peace would be found in the grave. The paratroopers went forward with renewed resolve, yet with a sense of grief and perhaps guilt that they had not been able to protect Devoe.

Zon, Holland, The Market Garden, Sunday Punch, September 17, 1944

When I told Russ the story, he shook his head as he often did and made the same frequently repeated remark. It was his solemn, emotional response of survivors guilt, "Why me? Why were the medics able to carry me back to safety when I was injured and so many had to be left behind?" Lest we forget, Devoe's death would be in vain.

Celebrating success in the Market Garden battle, WWII 70th Anniversary, Holland, 2014, one of the four (unidentified) women, reenactment depicts a 1944 nurse uniform. (Courtesy of friends, Tee and Rena Coleman.)

18
The Military Cadet Nursing Corps
— If Marjorie was a WWII Nurse

"Success in life has nothing to do with what you gain in life or accomplish for yourself.
It's what you do for others."
— *Danny Thomas*

Russ handed me a newspaper, May 6, 2004. He had just read that it was National Nurses Week and said, "Margie, thank you for your years of hard work." He pointed to a paragraph for me to read: "Your passion, humanity, dedication, and professionalism inspire and uplift us all. With head, hand, and heart you light up your patients lives. Thank you."

My twenty years as an intensive care unit nurse was nothing in difficulty compared to what it would have been in the Military Cadet Nursing Corps. Although I was only a two-year- old when Germany invaded Poland with a million troops, I was already saying, "I wanna be a nurse." I was just barely getting out of baby booties to start playing when Russ was fitting into his Army boots made to go to war and fight in. While I was crawling around under the dining room table and chairs obstacle course, Russ was crawling through the trenches of battle obstacles. The simple thank you Russ expressed for me when I was a nurse, made me

Lest We Forget

realize the appreciation he would have given the nurses who treated the wounded and cared for him while hundreds of wounded were being brought in during the Netherlands, Market Garden battle.

Intensive care nurses see more death and dying in a single day than most people do in a lifetime. The military nurses saw more. They were in the jungles, the European battlefield, and working in temporary, make-shift hospitals on the front lines of land and sea. The nurses were injured, killed, and became POW just like the men and officers.

America was caught off guard at Pearl Harbor with less than a thousand Honolulu nurses when thousands were needed instantly. By June, 1942, thanks to rapid, condensed training, there were 12,000 nurses in the Army Nurse Corps. They entered the Military as 2nd Lieutenants and if I could, I would have been one of them. Since the nurses badge looked a lot like a Generals, the Pfc. were often seen saluting a nurse, but it was the Pfc. who deserved the most respect and honor.

Marjorie Imagines Being in the Military Cadet Nursing Corps

I was taught to say I wanted to be a nurse ever since I learned to talk. When the "America Needs You" posters of attractive young women wearing Military Cadet Nursing Corps or American Red Cross uniforms, were pointing and saying "You

The Military Cadet Nursing Corps

are Needed Now," I quickly signed up. Everyone in America wanted to do their part and becoming a nurse was an opportunity to fulfill a dream and be of service. At the time there were not very many jobs for women on the battlefield. There were 400,000 women serving during WWII as range finders, radar operators, pilots and in numerous other work force positions. The 59,000 nurses saw more action and served in more locations than any other women.

Besides entering the intense rapid medical training, I was one of the nurses who had to get into shape physically as well. The nurses had to march with heavy packs, climb obstacle courses, and slide under barbwire fences, just like the troops. Joining the forces to serve the country as a nurse was not as ideal as I had hoped and I was surprised when the Nurse Corps was issued boots, helmets, and khaki uniforms instead of smart new white ones with a familiar nurses cap. Once in combat, many of the medical profession struggles of staff shortages and delayed delivery of supplies was the same as in any hospital, but the challenges were complicated with inability to have items ordered and delivered when needed. Medical personnel didn't know if the need was greater for food or blankets, beds or medicine. The nurses were in charge of orderly confusion that was completely unavoidable.

Would the smell of old blood, vomit, infection, or the shock and revulsion from constant painful screams cause the nurses to develop a blind, stoic indifference in their care, or would it be enough to challenge a nurse to risk her own life with

Lest We Forget

determination to save every serviceman she possibly could while they were in her care? The nurses brought their skills to battle, meeting the needs of the wounded, but perhaps love of country and inspiration acquired from the men was the motivation and strength to keep them going.

War nurses were doing their best under insurmountable conditions. Using the "ingenuity of a nurse" to save lives, the nurses quickly improvised surgical lights by hanging them from bombed out holes in the ceiling, makeshift surgical tables were made with doors taken off the hinges, and army knives were taken from dead bodies, sterilized, and used as surgical instruments.

The strength to carry on came from others. Nurses were in constant danger, felt helpless, completely exhausted, and near collapse, but they kept working. It was just a dream and a wish that I could change into a clean, white uniform and stiffly starched cap. Ideally the conditions would be in a modern hospital, with comfortable beds for the troops. The Cadet nurses realized that the Generals were to be feared, but the nurses Lieutenant badge represented the gentler, caring side of an officer as nurses tried to give each young man a little extra attention.

The nurse's role was never to diagnose, but to observe, record, evaluate, make wise medical assessments, and give the doctor accurate reports on the patient's condition. The physician's diagnosis for treatment came from the medical staff working together. The basis for orders to the nurses for care

The Military Cadet Nursing Corps

of the patients depended strongly on how efficiently and well they used their experience to evaluate the condition of the wounded.

Sending the servicemen back to their units, companies, and divisions as quickly as possible was of utmost importance in order to make room for the flow of the injured constantly being brought in. The patients arrived barely able to walk or be led in by a weak buddy. Some were brought in on heavy, awkward stretchers, or on the back and over the shoulder of a medic.

The only way to have any idea of what a war nurse experienced was if you've worked in an intensive care or emergency room during a major disaster. The paratrooper patients arrived unconscious, or collapsed unresponsive when they reached their destination. Upon examination, the injured were found with paralysis, hemorrhages, missing limbs, broken arms, compound fractures and in shock. Some of the patients had been trapped so long before being rescued that they were starved, dehydrated, too weak to respond, too battle worn to want to live, too unstable to be left alone. Because of the time elapsed before being treated, the blood soaked uniforms were stuck to the wounds and had to be soaked off or needed debridement. Some of the wounds smelled like rotten potatoes. Infected open wounds were worsened by pressure sores and there was little knowledge of how to treat it.

Cries and screams were heard: "Why did you rescue me? Why didn't they let me die on the battlefield? I can't take the pain. I want to die."

Lest We Forget

When one man saw his burned face reflected on a metal container he did not realize who it was. He was burnt beyond recognition and the nurse had to grab his hand to stop him from killing himself. He fought back yelling, "I can't live like this. I don't want anyone I know to see me like this."

Staggering and tired, I realized I had found an endurance and stamina that I did not know was within me. I had been working for 22 hours non-stop and finally stumbled to the door of the shattered, improvised hospital to grab a few breaths of bomb-smoke-filled "fresh air" when I heard a weakened voice mumble, "Margie, did you get my letter? Will you marry me?"

As Russ slipped back into unconsciousness, his was one stretcher I personally led into the evaluation triage treatment area to take care of myself. That was the most emotional, heart-felt, romantic proposal anyone could imagine.

When Russ survived the C-47 crash because of being moved to another plane and changed assignment, he decided to write Margie, the Cadet Nurse he got to know in London after his injury in France. He was missing out on some of the things in life that mattered the most. He missed companionship and his shared values with someone else. While driving the Army motorcycle during the changed assignment, Russ ended up with another injury that almost killed him. Russ wondered how many times his life was spared that he did not even know about. Now he was back under medical care with a severe concussion that caused him to be in

The Military Cadet Nursing Corps

and out of consciousness. Russ didn't remember how he got there or where he was. His pupils were unequal, his vitals were still unstable because the 88mm blew up beside him, and he was thrown into the air and across the field so far and with such force and impact that he was bruised, bleeding and facing closed head trauma.

From England, Marjorie was transferred to help transport seriously injured servicemen from the massive destruction and horrendous injuries in Holland to an improvised, temporary hospital. The paratroopers were admitted into the facility where mass surgical suites were set up, row upon row of patients waited for care, and assembly areas were turned into units for 20 patients per room. When Russ arrived, Marjorie hardly recognized him. He had seen more tragedy, more killings and dead bodies, felt more pain, and heard more terror than anyone should have to.

After a few days of treatment, including some healthy food and fluids, overseen of course with some special TLC from his private duty nurse (me), I accepted his proposal and we decided to have a military wedding. The ingenuity of a nurse works in mysterious ways, and the nurses went to work helping prepare for a wedding. From an old torn Air Corp white silk parachute, a group of nurses started to hand sew a wedding dress. Remnants from the parachute were used to make large bows and gathers around the hemline. The parachute's puckered vents were used for pleats and the holes for thin parachute cords to be laced down the back

Lest We Forget

stitching. They designed strips of white silk to be open for a veil. Surprisingly, it turned out to be a beautiful wedding dress, instead of a Halloween costume. Cut off khaki military pant leg strips from the shorter nurses' uniforms were twisted around twigs to make artificial flowers for a bouquet. It had to be completely original and unique, fit for a military wedding! Each thing made was a one of a kind design just for me and I could not have been more pleased!

A rare, imaginary military wedding needed equal thought and time to be put into the ceremony. The importance of creating a positive force for the future meant remembering a world with our happiest memories, recalling the best things from our past. If we could, we would dance as if at a prom on a reception floor covered with rose petals, but Russ was confined to his cot. If we could, the church steeple would ring out with bells and a small choir of voices would sing, a group of string chamber musicians would be playing, but instead, the wedding would be in an improvised emergency hospital. That meant they would open the windows and listen to the chit-chat serenading choir of bird songs. If the people of England and across Europe could sing in a bomb shelter, the doctors, nurses, and patients would certainly be able to sing along together with the comforting words of "Amazing Grace." The sun would come out tomorrow. Birds could still sing and flowers would grow again. Children voices would return to school and play

The Military Cadet Nursing Corps

again without hearing the sound of air raids and bombs blasting in the air above them.

On the day of our wedding, Russ was still very weak, unable to be up for very long, and just as we feared, the ceremony would have to be at his bedside. Crowded around him, the nurses stood in as bridesmaids and doctors represented Groomsmen. I walked between the rows of patients like I would have been walking down the aisle of a church. The injured were the cheering airborne witnesses and wedding guests. When I walked past the paratroopers, they laughed in appreciation realizing the designer gown was made of silk fabric from a parachute. The rip cords were laced and hanging down my back, instead of around satin covered wedding gown buttons.

The chaplain began with some meaningful, romantic comments to make us plan for a bright future: "Did you see it – the gentle breeze from the flutter of a butterfly's wings? Did you taste it – the first-ripened fresh ear of sweet corn from an Indiana farm field? Did you smell it – a freshly baked all-American apple pie? Did you feel it – the touch of a newborn baby's hand wrapped around your little finger?"

Personalizing who we were, he continued, "Marjorie was born in the Blue Bonnet, oil State of Texas and Russ is a Hoosier, born in Indiana, the land known for corn and basketball, but it took a big fight to get them together. It is called WWII. Russell and Marjorie both seem to like meeting in a hospital. The first time was in a London hospital after the

Lest We Forget

Normandy Invasion. Today they are back together in a bomb-torn, improvised hospital in Eindhoven, after the 101st Airborne jumped into Holland. Their honeymoon view is out the bomb-blasted hole in a wall window where, from Russ's bed, he can wake up daily and see the results of battle. Russ had been writing to Marjorie, not knowing she had been transferred here. The letters had not yet been forwarded, but in his subconscious state Russ recognized Marjorie when he was brought to our offhand hospital after his second injury. And, now let me make this official."

Two officers held their rifles arched across each side of the bed, where I had squeezed in close beside Russ. We were both smiling admirably at each other and then prepared for our vows.

"Would you repeat after me? I, Marjorie Anne Delafield, do take thee, Francis Russell Snell, to be my lawful wedded husband, for better or for worse, in sickness and in health, from this day forward, until death do us part."

"And now, Paratrooper, would you repeat after me? I, Francis Russell Snell, do take thee, Marjorie, to be my lawful wedded wife, for better or for worse, in sickness and in health, from this day forward, until death do us part."

During a war, there was something more solemn and sacred about the value for life, recognizing the need for God's blessings and protection. Appreciation for the meaning of prayer for peace in a military wedding seemed more meaningful than at an expensive wedding in a

The Military Cadet Nursing Corps

beautifully decorated chapel, formal sanctuary, or large church. There would be no honeymoon or celebrating at a reception, because the wedding guests needed to have their treatments and medications, Russ included. The doctors and nurses, myself included, had to get back to work.

I had to rush from the ceremony to change out of my parachute gown and into my khaki uniform to get back on duty. Russ and I were aware that the few who were married during the war had no special privileges. We would have to live in separate barracks when Russ was discharged. That news was not as difficult to take as when Russ was informed that he would be transferred immediately to a hospital in Paris once he was stable. When I heard of their decision, I assumed there must be complications that I had not been told of, and so I looked at the medical records overnight. Nausea, dizziness, and vomiting meant that Russ had a severe concussion, possibly complicated with bleeding "closed head trauma." I requested a transfer to accompany Russ to the hospital in Paris, but the request was denied.

I tried to pull rank, and said, "I'm a 2nd Lieutenant."

"Of course," they laughed at me and said, "All nurses are."

"Yes, I know," I apologized, "but I just got married. I'm concerned about my husband and I have been on the front line long enough. Send someone else here for a while and I will return when

Lest We Forget

it's my turn again. Who can I talk to and appeal your decision?"

The request was approved and although at different times and different routes, Russ and I met up again at the military hospital in Paris. Russ began to improve. Being back to civilization where he could actually look out his hospital room window and see the beauty of the Paris skyline and the Eiffel Tower was healing in itself. With that view, we could imagine the honeymoon we never had.

I was never more proud that I chose to be a nurse than when I imagined marrying my hero who was never more handsome than when he proposed to me in his weakened, semiconscious condition while being admitted for medical care! Our hypothetical relationship was based on friendship, empathy, and understanding that progressed as realistically as in real life, 45 years later.

Although the information about myself is my "what if" imaginary story as a nurse, the Military Cadet Nursing Corps information and details about Russ are as true and close to reality as possible, lest we forget the emotions of living through the injuries and stress on those who cared for and experienced the scars of war.

The Military Cadet Nursing Corps

Marjorie A. Delafield Tomlin graduated as a Registered Nurse, June, 1962. F. Russell Snell surprised her when she got off work, 1989, and took this photograph of her wearing a modern nurses uniform, sitting on the bumper of her Mercury Cougar!

19
Bastogne, Battle of the Bulge
— Russ's Value for Life and Fear of Death
December 19, 1944

"The outstanding courage and resourcefulness and undaunted determination of this gallant force is in keeping with the highest traditions of the service."
— *By command of Lieutenant General Patton: Hobart R. Gay, Brigadier General of the U. S. Army Chief of Staff*

Reims, France population was growing again by leaps and bounds as the paratroopers gathered together in preparation for the next phase of the war. Russ and other injured soldiers were being discharged from hospitals and returned to their units. Others were returning from England where they had gone to await their next orders. It was bitter sweet for Russ to rejoin Charlie Company. He was thankful to have survived, but in utter dismay to find out how few there were who he recognized. The 101st 506 paratroopers had another 178 of their men killed in Holland.

Large numbers of replacements arrived while Russ was in the hospital, but there was no time for him to get acquainted or enjoy a good night-before-battle fancy meal. It came as a simple order to report for duty, bring your back pack, follow directions, and pile into the back of an Army truck.

Lest We Forget

The 506 paratroopers were left to wonder where their parachutes, ammunition, and supplies were.

It didn't take long to realize how cold it was going to be. Not even the body heat of the troops could warm them as they huddled and crowded together. There didn't seem to be any difference in the ability to survive a too hot summer or a too cold winter. Perhaps that was a big reason paratroopers received the $50.00 a month more pay. While I was thinking about the hell of a Bastogne blizzard that Russ had experienced, I remembered my mild (in comparison) weather conditions during my childhood from a gift package I received in the mail from a friend.

The gift was a bent, rusty old horse shoe nailed to a weathered fence board hanging from barbwire and decorated with torn red bandana strips. It had been posted on the side of a barn door next to the coiled rope of a Texas cowboy. The words were roughly painted to read:

Texas Werken Cowpokes Wether Fercaster. Jest hang yer garanteed akurat fercaster outside and foller theze drecshuns:

1. If its wet its a rainin! Caint werk in the rain
2. If its wite its a snowin! Its too dang cold ta werk.

Bastogne, Battle of the Bulge

3. If it berns yer hand its too hot to werk. Best find yer some shade and cold beer.

4. If its a swangin -that dern winds a blowin – its not safe to werk with them cow pies a flyin'

5. If yer tercastors gone beter git werkin on gettin a posse cause theres a dang bandit loose.

When the paratroopers trucks came to a halt, the men bailed out by jumping onto the cold hard earth instead of from a plane as they were trained to glide, then roll on impact. As the men started to march, there was no reason to deny the fear they felt. General George S. Patton, Jr. said that "Wars may be fought with weapons, but they are won by men." The paratroopers were reminded that courage was the act of being the only one who knew you were scared to death.

Men of the 506 restored their courage by remembering they were fighting for mom's apple pie, peach cobbler, or in Russ's case, the memory of his mother's cornbread and beans. While marching, many paratroopers recalled having their hope restored from words in the scriptures, Isaiah 40:31, to walk and don't faint. After all, they were Screaming Eagles and the Bible reference admonished them to "Mount up with wings as Eagles, run and not be weary, walk and not faint."

Lest We Forget

Those were the things that helped them to put one foot in front of the other, because they remembered many of their buddies who couldn't. The ones who were unable to take another single step were dead. Those who remained had to go and do it for those who couldn't.

While marching towards Bastogne, injured men fell to the ground and it was a horrendous shock to see so many dying in trenches or beside the road when there was nowhere to bury them. Struggling forward, the paratroopers witnessed the result of men who had fallen, instantly freezing in horrible positions just as they had dropped in awkward body contortions.

The 101st were disheartened, but refused to be discouraged. In desperation and frustration, some of the Band of Brothers threw their empty canteens out into the snow. Russ said, "One thing we didn't throw away was our helmets, because we were hoping that we would be able to cook or warm a meal in them. We were praying for a C-47 to drop food packs, like Manna from Heaven."

As the paratroopers advanced, they were constantly looking and listening for a U. S. air drop of desperately needed supplies, perhaps more necessary than food. They were starved, frostbitten, and confused. Men began to wonder if it was another mistake (like being dropped in the wrong location on D-Day). They thought someone must have failed to report where to send their equipment.

Bastogne, Battle of the Bulge

At one point the ammunition ration was only eleven rounds to a gun.

Russ thought again of the difference in the sound of a German and American airplane. He said, "When we heard a surge, followed with a dull sound, it was the Germans, but when there was one steady, long, loud hum, we knew it was one of us, one of ours."

That was another way of staying focused, to keep their ears open and be prepared to dash for cover. When there was nowhere to find a place to hide, they had to try desperately to dig holes in the ground for cover. Some of the paratroopers could not run because they suffered from frost bite that resulted in permanent damage to hands and feet. The temperature was 17 degrees. In some pockets, the temperature was less and the ground itself was frozen and impossible to dig into. The howling wind plastered the snow against their blistered faces and it was difficult to think of things to do to stay alive, but they were determined to survive and fulfill their rendezvous with destiny. The sound of an American plane would renew their purpose to not be warmongering fighters putting on a show. They were there to end the war.

Under Field Marshall Karl von Rundstadt's direction, the German forces in Bastogne included the attack by five full Divisions and over 1000 German tanks. Their full intent and objective was to advance full force on the 101st Airborne, keeping the

Lest We Forget

seven highways and one railroad open for the German army. One of America's youngest generals, was forty-six-year-old Brigadier General Anthony C. McAuliffe who was severely outnumbered with a mere 10,000 men. He was acting commander of the 101st Airborne Division with the addition of "odds and ends" of the U. S. Army's ninth and tenth Armored Divisions.

Through panic, terror, and shock, the 101st fought on. Words cannot describe how tired the men were. When most of us have a rare night with only three or four hours of sleep, we think that's being tired, but going for days in pain, fatigue, stress, and staggering from freezing sleeplessness and starvation, that's tired.

Through the most bloody defense and counter offensive that Russ experienced, elements of the 506, 1st Battalion suffered the heaviest loss, January 10, 1945. They took direct artillery fire from German tanks during the siege in the Hamlet of Foy where Joe Reed was platoon leader of Company C. The Germans were seen sleeping as scattered silhouettes across the white snow, easily seen targets for the paratroopers to pick them off, but Joe could not believe his eyes when he found 100 German tanks. It looked like half of the German tank brigade idling their motors. He commanded, "Let's get the hell out of here." They headed back towards Noville, for what he thought would be the

Bastogne, Battle of the Bulge

slaughter to begin. Still short of equipment he said, "All we had were rifles – nothing to stop a tank."

During one of the memorable December, 1944 occurrences in Bastogne, Jim Cadden knew of a make-shift crew who he could put together to take over an abandoned Sherman, German tank from the Nazi 10th Armored Division. Cadden managed to find enough men to man the controls, but started searching desperately because he had not been able to find a driver. Finally one trooper volunteered his services, claiming he could drive a tank.

At first the abandoned tank would not start, finally it lunged forward, but would not steer. From the turret, Cadden was screaming, "Stop this thing," as the unidentified paratrooper driver drove it straight through a thick brick building.

"I thought you said you could drive a tank," Cadden continued to yell.

Wishing he had stuck to parachuting and marching, the embarrassed trooper said, "Well, Sir, I thought it would drive the same. Back home on the farm, I could drive a tractor."

The 101st reached their objective, but their boots were frozen, their food supply was depleted and they had no strength left. The Germans knew of the paratroopers weakened, starved, scarred condition and proceeded to completely encircle, drawn up in a siege ring around the airborne. That led to the battle becoming known as the Hole in the

Lest We Forget

Doughnut, the Battle of the Bulge. The Nazi army had forgotten the tenacity of the Americans to never give up.

The German Commander demanded an ultimatum to surrender immediately, because they knew the Americans were completely surrounded. Young Brigadier General McAuliffe, December 22, 1944, answered immediately and boldly with one simple, now famous word, "Nuts."

That unexpected response was confusing to the Germans, but when the American troops heard that their Commander had said, "Nuts," it became the regrouping, reviving symbol that boosted their morale in time for Patton's arrival. Back home, Americans started using the comment and it became the WWII phrase equally meaningful as in Texas, to "Remember the Alamo."

Lest we forget, the Battle of the Bulge was during a very cold Christmas holiday, the paratroopers certainly lacked a bulge of presents. Their attitude and holiday spirit was an example of a lesson we need to be reminded of, that it's not the size or number of presents that make the day meaningful. A small group of the troops profited from the actions of a few nurses who presented them with a Christmas eve gift. Remnants and pieces of shiny metal objects that the nurses had found, along with the help of a few of their officers working together, shaped stars and decorative Christmas symbols into ornaments. Discarded

Bastogne, Battle of the Bulge

empty gasoline canisters confiscated from the German tanks were used to cut and form into a very distorted replica of a Christmas tree.

Some of the paratroopers had never before seen snow and under different circumstances the beauty of the landscape would have been breathtaking, but it was covered with trails of blood; and war tanks completely surrounded them. The only thing left that could take their breath was when they received a one day after Christmas army plane drop of some desperately needed food rations.

It took an extraordinary kind of willingness to do everything possible, beyond their knowledge and training, to keep going. Once they knew help was on its way, the suffering paratroopers maintained their bravery, tenacity, fortitude and endurance. They were fearless soldiers who believed in each other even when completely outnumbered and surrounded. American soldiers didn't want to die, but they were willing to. They would continue to fight at all cost, until the last ounce of strength and life was left in them.

The courageous attitude of a paratrooper required stronger, tougher leaders than the men. General George Patton Jr. was that kind of man when he arrived December 27, 1944. He was described as being bold, resolute, and duty bound. He believed in victory at all cost and so there was no time for fear. The other officers were afraid of Patton because he demanded perfection, but the

Lest We Forget

troops respected him because he was their kind of officer. He led by example. They knew exactly what he meant when he said, "I'm not training you to die for your country. I'm training you for other men to die for theirs."

Patton's army would have the ability and courage to go beyond all human possibility. He inspired the paratroopers with toughness. The 101st had already gone beyond expectations, but under these circumstances, Patton would demand more. He was the one sent in as the last defense in Bastogne and he had a plan with a strategy that was clear, definite, simple and would not fail: to "Attack, attack, attack, and then attack again."

When Patton spoke to his men the expectations were to, "Be the best fighters in the world, not to defend but to attack. Use the first attack to advance. Move. Move. Move. Do what's not expected. Victory at all cost."

The 101st together with parts of the strong, powerful U. S. Third Army's ninth, tenth, and the 80th Divisions were sent in hurriedly to ward off the Germans attack. The combined efforts of the Americans had maintained their stronghold beyond the Germans expectations because they knew they had the Americans cornered, trapped and strongly outnumbered. They thought the U. S. had no chance to survive.

The fighting was continuous, but the American army refused to surrender because of the

Bastogne, Battle of the Bulge

strong leadership of President Roosevelt, General Patton and their own Brigadier General McAuliffe. Russ was again seriously injured from the blast of another 88mm explosion beside the foxhole from which he was fighting. There are no atheists in a foxhole. January 16, 1945, Russ was blown out of the hole where he was fighting from and again he was knocked unconscious, but by the grace of God, he would survive.

There were some beautiful, peaceful sounding names that brought back good memories of the once tranquil towns as they were before the war: from the base of a hill in Noville, the Hamlet of Foy (which changed hands a minimum of six times), perhaps it was by truck from Alsace-Lloraine where some paratroopers had returned and been victorious. The names were meaningless words unless that was where Company C or others from the 506 were located. Russ said, "All I knew about was what was happening right where I was and what I was doing. Not until the war was practically over did I hear about what was going on around us." Although in small groups, paratroopers knew they were fighting together as one, no matter where or how far away the others were.

Bastogne became known as the Gettysberg of WWII. There were 77,000 casualties in the Battle of the Bulge, but both Bastogne and Gettysburg were historical turning points. Each serviceman performed extraordinary acts of heroism and

Lest We Forget

gallantry, but most of their stories were buried with the men who died or found the experience too difficult to talk about.

At last when victory in Bastogne was achieved at all costs, the 101st, 506 were withdrawn by train to Mourmelon le Petit. The exhausted men Marched in Review for General Dwight Eisenhower who presented them with the Presidential Unit Citation, the first such award ever offered. The high honor was equivalent to the Distinguished Service Cross as would have been given individually. The prestigious award was more meaningful to them as a whole than if bestowed individually because the men of Currahee fought alone, but eternally would be known for working together as one. They would always deny that any one of them was exceptional above any of the rest.

The instructors believed that personally having to pack their own parachute would make the paratroopers respect and have confidence in the parachute. Learning the parachute parts and how the 26-28 foot diameter could be wrapped to fit into a shoulder back-pack and could be activated by the static line from the ceiling of the C-47 rather than from a rip cord. The parachute itself was designed with 28 silk panels, encircled at the apex with an elastic banded "pucker vent." The control during descent was guided with break-cord suspension lines and a ridged frame attached to the rear harness, completely enclosing the canopy.

Bastogne, Battle of the Bulge

Jumping required the accuracy of crouching near the door, with the right foot slightly ahead of the other and the hands shoulder high on the outside of the C-47 door. Equally important was to vigorously push off and leap outside the door. That elastic banded "pucker vent" at the highest point of the parachute had an important, meaningful significance to Russ!

General Patton was a man with a well-defined attitude of blood and guts. He accepted that profanity was just troop language. Of course, Russ laughed when I compared him to Patton. I explained to him, "Russ, you and Patton both loved the desert because it's healthy, dry, and requires endurance! Patton accepted that war profanity was appropriate and although you do not swear, you say, 'Blow it out your puckered vent' when you're upset."

Patton said of Desert Summit, where he trained one million servicemen, that it was, "The place where God forgot," but Russ was glad to forget the Indiana snow. He said, "I no longer have to shovel and plow, living here in Patton's desert!"

Patton chose the training site near an aqueduct where it was necessary to acquire a permit prior to tapping into for use. When the request was met with delay and opposition that was wasting his time, Patton said, "We're already tapped in so take as long as you want to issue the permit."

Lest We Forget

Patton's toughness inspired the men, but he also had a softer, tender side that sometimes brought him to tears. I've always felt about Russ's eyes when they moistened emotionally, that it takes a strong man to show his tears. Patton had a high emotional state witnessing the devastating wounds of war and accepted the profanity of men who had earned a right to anger. Russ was also in a high emotional state being one of the injured and found his own acceptable way to express it.

I never found another person or book that used the phrase, but all of Russ's friends and family knew that when he said, "Blow it out your puckered vent," he was pretty upset. We knew that Russ's expression was similar to McAuliffe saying, "Nuts."

The words mean, "Are you kidding? You're crazy. No way. You don't know what you're talking about. You don't know who you're talking to. You've got your nerve. Never. When hell freezes over," or worse.

When Russ left by truck on December 19, 1944, to the 506 Infantry's undisclosed location of Bastogne, he found relief when Patton arrived December 27. Russ continued to fight until January 16, 1945. It was after almost a month of continuous battle when Russ was blown out of a foxhole and experienced his third injury. He had earned a Purple Heart and his second Oak Leaf Cluster: one from each battle of Normandy, the Netherlands, and Bastogne. He was alive and still

Bastogne, Battle of the Bulge

had in his pocket that piece of parachute from his jump into Normandy.

It was late and our family reunion had come to the "end of a perfect day," sharing the inspiration of Russ's life. I thought he might tell us all he'd had enough and to blow it out our puckered vent, but instead he thoughtfully wanted to tell us all, "Don't thank me. Thank every serviceman you meet for their service. We do it for all of our family to live in peace and freedom. We even do it for those who don't appreciate the freedoms we have."

I gave each one of our family an important packet of information about the 101st, 506, Company C story after Bastogne. It was the rest of the story, going on to Landsberg concentration camp, the Berghof, and Eagles Nest. Because of his injury, Russ could not go on with his Band of Brothers. There would be no paratroopers if there were no parachutes, just as I would not be the wife of a WWII veteran if there was no war. The paratroopers learned to love and respect their chute just as I cherished my favorite hero, Russ.

When the airborne started their training jumps, they had to trust that the professional instructor had packed their parachutes correctly. The paratroopers spent hours learning to pack their own chute and knew they were entirely on their own for jumps from the towers and five training jumps from the C-47. Each man had to do it meticulously correct or they could jump to their

Lest We Forget

death if they made a mistake. Next, they developed trust in each other to pack their parachute for each other. They had confidence that they would do it right for each other so that when they grabbed a parachute from the stack, there would be no fear or hesitation whether the parachute was safe for combat jumps.

Russ gave us confidence and reassurance that he did it for us. He felt vulnerable and all alone in the chute he had packed for himself, but by the time he jumped in combat, his Band of Brothers had jumped together as one in parachutes that were packed for each other. Russ's long life was spent packing his chute for us and helping others. That is why he is my hero, an American hero, a national treasure.

He kept that symbol of taking responsibility for himself so that he could say to us, "I did it for YOU with the hope that you will not have to do it alone. The lives of so many were lost for the sake of our freedom, but because my life was spared, I will say every time I see you, I love you yet today and I packed my chute for the sake of your freedom. I packed your chute. We stand together."

20
From Landsberg Liberators to the Eagles Nest
— Russ Injured, Unable to Proceed

"I hate war as only a soldier who has lived it can; only as one who has seen its brutality."
— General Dwight D. Eisenhower,
President

For closure on an important part of the 506, Company C legacy, walk with them through the halls of the Holocaust Museum, Washington DC, 2006. Because of the age and health of the last eight veterans who could attend, their reunion was held in the nation's Capitol so that we could visit two important places unique to their history, the recently completed WWII Memorial and the Holocaust Museum. The experience was personalized when each of us stepped into the museum and received an identification card with a photograph of an actual victim of the Holocaust that we could individually identify with. The bold print included the Jewish person's name, place of birth, and date of death. We were instructed to wear a yellow star, marking each of us as a Jew.

The paratroopers and family members were walking among other groups of shocked people who looked in disbelief and reacted to the experiences of displaced persons being loaded into trains trans-

Lest We Forget

porting them to concentration camps. Each of us carried through the halls the weight of that name and photograph in our hand. Through the emotional experience we walked with a gut-wrenching feeling and heart-breaking silence. During the tour some people were literally sick to their stomach. We witnessed the reality in film that showed identification tattoo numbers on the arm of discriminated people labeled as inferior and we saw the reality of actual shoes, toys, journals, and ID papers that survived the holocaust, but the people didn't. There was hardly a dry eye.

Norm Smith, our Company C reunion clerk, was being pushed in his wheel chair and looking specifically for one thing in particular. As he slowly worked his way through the museum, he carried the extra weight on his shoulders of the images in his mind of the Camp that C Company was involved with. We witnessed all of the Concentration Camp names etched into the walls throughout the halls of the museum and at long last Norm saw the name he was looking for, etched in the surface of a window. Landsberg.

In an area west of Munich, Landsberg was the haunt of perhaps 20, but one in particular established, formidable prison knows as "The Fortress." Once incarcerated there for his failure to overthrow Bavaria, Hitler elevated the site as an elated shrine to himself, the intensely admired German Chancellor.

From Landsberg Liberators to the Eagles Nest

Historically known as the location where Hitler, the jailed recluse, wrote his "Mein Kampf" struggles, it was more memorable to the 101st, 506, Company C paratroopers as being the Landsberg concentration camp. The Fortress was part of the Kaufering complex of 11 camps administered by Dachau. Kaufering IV was uncovered by the men of C Company shortly after many of the prisoners were sent on a death march towards Dachau when the German guards recognized that the U. S. troops were nearing. The facility was set on fire, burning to death an estimated 250-500 inmates who were too ill and weak to walk. Landsberg was the strongest reminder to the 101st that sulphur was the smell of dead bodies. The thought is grizzly beyond belief that innocent human beings would be burned, maimed, raped and beaten to their death. Newborn babies were thrown into the air to be stabbed to death with daggers thrown at their defenseless, helpless, vulnerable little bodies.

While visiting with the Smiths during the reunion, Norm spoke of the talk he had given about the holocaust and I asked him if he would mind sending us a copy of what he had written. As soon as it arrived in the mail we read it and then immediately called to thank him. "Norm, we just received the packet of all the information you sent, including your touching, emotional talk. Thanks for keeping all of the 506 Company C records. To your credit that documentation is why the members of

Lest We Forget

the 101st, Company C are known as the Liberators of Landsberg. I have a question, or request. Would you mind if I told or passed on your story to others?"

Norm humbly responded, "You may use it at any time, in any way you choose to inform and educate everyone possible. It's a painful story, but it must be retold and passed on to future generations."

Norm Smith's story cannot be condensed, improved or embellished. It needs to be told exactly as it was given and so it is repeated in its entirety just as he wrote and spoke it for the first time at the Omaha Community om Hashoah Commemoration Service at the Beth Israel Synagogue in Omaha, Nebraska, May 4, 2005. His title, lest we forget, the "Recollections of a Liberator:"

> "As evidenced by my appearance here tonight, I have the humble honor of presenting the Liberators of 1945. As a result of time, place, and circumstances, I survived whereas, other Liberators I represent, either fell in battle, live today as crippled and maimed residents of VA homes and hospitals, or are living as you are with the vivid memory of a war which ended 60 years ago. The magnitude of the Holocaust cannot be

From Landsberg Liberators to the Eagles Nest

accurately described by the reflections of a single Liberator. What I contribute tonight is but a minute piece of the truth as I witnessed it in April, 1945.

"I am a retired educator. I frequently spoke to high school students and general audiences about The Holocaust. When I did, I used a paraphrase in Future Shock, 1967, written by Alvin Toffler, words to the effect, "Students without knowledge of the past see nothing unusual about the present." Thus, I said to young people, 'If you have no knowledge of The Holocaust, you will see nothing unusual about the present activities of those who deny it and call it a hoax.'

"April 28, 1945: Enroute to Landsberg, Germany, I am a young 20-year-old soldier. We are in a truck convoy with tanks leading. We can hear the fighting but are too far back to actually see the encounter. Only as we slowly advance can we review the fresh results of battle. We enter a thick pall of smoke. It clings to the highway. There is a putrid, pungent odor that nauseates many of us. We cannot see. The convoy seems to slip

Lest We Forget

ahead almost out of sight at times. Finally we come to the source, a burning, smoldering building. The word is passed along the column. The building was packed with human beings barricaded, doused in gasoline, and set afire. This is our introduction to The Holocaust!

"Here I digress for a few moments. Thirty years passed before surviving members of my WWII company would decide to have reunions. At these affairs old memories are often recalled, discussed, and argued. I can find only one member who remembers the smoke. Could I have just imagined that event? I searched for an answer and in 1969 I found vindication. The source was a TIME-LIFE book series called "This Fabulous Century...1940-50, Vol. V, p131. An anonymous G. I. wrote "Somewhere in Germany, 1945:"

"Since seeing you in England I have sort of covered three more countries: France, Germany and Austria. I've seen what wasn't ever

From Landsberg Liberators to the Eagles Nest

meant for human eyes to see. We were in Landsberg, Hitler's cell where he wrote "Mein Kampf." Dachau was close by. Have you ever seen stacks and piles of HUMAN bodies...200-300 in each pile, sprawled out, starved and beaten and gassed to death?

The only thing I've seen to compare with it was at the Landsberg camp. The evening before we moved in they had put 250 people, men and women, into this house which was sort of half dug in. The house was then saturated with gasoline and a match was all that was necessary.

The next morning we moved in. But it didn't smell like ordinary smoke. Have you ever smelled human flesh burning? That was it!!!

Lest We Forget

> We now have an outfit that cannot smell any sort of fire without that incident passing through his mind. It seems that it will never leave us. Never."

"In 1985, shortly after I [Norm Smith] spoke at a ceremony at the state Capitol which included the mention of the Landsberg camp, I received a phone call. The call originated at Lodgepole, Nebraska. The caller was E. K. Yanney who identified himself as the president of the local bank. He commented to wit, 'Landsberg! I haven't heard anyone talk about Landsberg since the battle. I was in one of the tanks ahead of you.'

"Soon we arrived at the gates of the Landsberg camp. The Germans have been using slave labor to build an underground jet plane factory. The gates have been flung open. Everywhere you look are the dead, the dying, and the surviving. Those who are able are milling around. Some remain inside the fence, afraid to

From Landsberg Liberators to the Eagles Nest

come out. They are gaunt, skin-covered skeletons. There is a certain wild, glassy, vacant stare about their eyes which even a faint smile cannot alter.

"We are stunned and dumbfounded. We look at the survivors in disbelief. They in turn are staring at us unable to believe that the moment called freedom is theirs. We call out searching for anyone who can speak English. One person steps forward and identifies himself as an Austrian banker who has been imprisoned for eight years. He demonstrates the extent of the emaciation of his body by placing his hands near his crotch, then extending his fingers to completely encircle his leg. There is room to spare. From him we hear about diet and starvation rations. We seriously err by giving him food which he vomits. His body weight is probably 60-80 pounds. Only medical intervention can save him.

"As we are being assembled and directed to conduct a search of the nearby woods, an old man with a stick over his shoulder makes his way through the crowd. At the end of the

Lest We Forget

stick is a rag pouch which no doubt contains something he values. He passes by me and heads down a nearby road. I watch with interest because he is an exception. He is definitely leaving; only he knows where. About 50-60 yards down the road I see him stop, go over to the shoulder and ditch, sit down to rest, the stick still tightly held and projected over the shoulder. I dismiss him from my mind and we begin to sweep the woods.

"The woods in this part of Germany have been re-forested. The trees are evenly spaced, row on row. There is little underbrush and underfoot the thick bed of pine needles makes the ground soft. There are pools and pools of human excrement. The inmates have diarrhea and they leave a trail in the woods. Every few yards it seems there is a prone figure lying still with a ragged garment pulled up around and over the head. I use the muzzle of my rifle to left the garment and pose the face. They are all the same—dead. They have found a place to die with a certain degree of dignity.

From Landsberg Liberators to the Eagles Nest

"As we complete our sweep, I enter what appears to be an administration building. Inside are several inmates rummaging. They freeze in place when they hear the noise I make behind them. Slowly they turn their heads and look at me. It is as if I were a puppeteer and that I could control them by strings. They are relieved to see that I am an American. I wave; they wave back and smile. I return to the main gate.

"We are stepping in, around, and over corpses. The stench is overwhelming. Many of us find a place to vomit. I start down the road the old man traveled. He is still sitting there. Over an hour has passed and he has not moved. When I am closer I realize he is dead also, but still sitting, still clutching his precious stick and pouch.

"April 29, 1945. I was sent on other mopping-up patrols, but I knew what the rest of my company did. Company C this day rounded up civilians from Landsberg and force-marched them from the city to the camp. They denied any knowledge of

Lest We Forget

the existence of the camp. Few would admit having been a Nazi.

"We have been ordered on to another objective: this time an attack upon the National Redoubt. This area was touted as the place where Hitler would make his final stand. It contained the town of Berchtesgaden and nestled in the surrounding mountains was his famed home, The Berghof. There were reputed to be some 1,500 SS troops in barracks there. On May 5th the 506 Parachute Infantry entered Berchtesgaden meeting little resistance. On May 8th my platoon was occupying the Berghof and it was there we learned that the war in Europe had ended."

Norman Smith's talk was 60 years after WWII, but those attending still had expressions of grief and pain on their face as though it was 1945. Norm told the audience what he had spent his life doing: educating his students of the Holocaust tragedy, and that we can never let the murder of millions of Jews, any religion, race or nationality, ever happen again. Norman continued his talk:

From Landsberg Liberators to the Eagles Nest

TEACHING ABOUT THE HOLOCAUST

"Whenever I received the invitation to join a classroom teacher in planning objectives, I asked that teacher to share with me what the class had been studying. In the beginning the most common units of study were centered around The Diary of Anne Frank supplemented by films, documentaries, books, and U. S. Army archival materials. This was before the ADL distributed organized Holocaust studies units and materials.

"Immediately after the war ended every GI in Europe who wished to pack up war trophies could do so and ship these home free. All items bearing the Swastika were declared legal prizes of war. All boxes had to be inspected before shipment. All munitions and automatic weapons were restricted. Items shipped home as souvenirs became valuable teaching tools. Thus, my role in team teaching was to display my artifacts and be certain that every student could pick up any item and handle it. A student might examine the SS Death Head insignia up close. I had a silver-framed picture of Hitler taken

Lest We Forget

from under the BERGHOF which was given as a personal gift to various dignitaries as awards.

"Sixty years ago the major part of my life was yet to be lived. I knew from the first that I would never leave the memories of Landsberg behind. I did not know that the onset of Polio at age 26 would persuade me to become a teacher. I did not know that my sensitivity to The Holocaust would lead me to become a collector of Holocaust materials. I did not know that I and others like me would bear the title of LIBERATORS. I came to realize that there were other LIBERATORS like myself who were also collectors and who also welcomed the chance to speak in schools. Like all collectors we traded materials, loaned each other photos, records and shared experiences. I met many unusual persons.

"On one occasion years ago I was showing slides taken at Dachau. The classroom teacher had also invited Father Flisiak. He was a Polish priest imprisoned at Dachau for 8 years. He was at that time the parish priest at Krakow, Nebraska. When I

From Landsberg Liberators to the Eagles Nest

showed a picture of the crematorium building there he said, 'I carried bags of cement used to build that building.'

"When I accepted this invitation to speak to you tonight, I also made it known to many teachers who at one time invited me to join them as a support person in presenting the truths about the Holocaust. There are a number of my old colleagues here tonight. This is a very incomplete roster and the years have robbed me of many others I should mention. Nonetheless, my hope has always been that as teachers we made a lasting impact upon the students we shared.

"And so I say to young people in Toffler's words: 'If you are ignorant of the knowledge of the past, you will see nothing unusual about the present when so-called hate groups and revisionists attempt to re-write history without the Holocaust.' I tell these kinds of persons that, all who know, all who were there, survivor and liberator, have left a legacy of writings, oral histories, motion pictures, photographs and artifacts in repositories. And finally I tell all that there

Lest We Forget

> are two things we cannot leave them: One, is the memory of the stink and stench of the dead and dying, and the other is the sound, sounds of people in the throes of death."

How do you explain tears for ones you never knew? There's such a fine line between life and death when both are within a breath away. How do you go on? The only way for Americans was with values for life and the pursuit of happiness, that every man was created equal. No one should die alone. We entered WWII because no one should have to sit alone, be alone, walk alone through the shadow of death. There should be nowhere on earth where bombs stripped trees of their leaves, leaving the mighty oak without it's relaxing shade or where no popular waving poplars are left standing to billow in the breeze. Survivors believed that sunset was either an insult or hope that the sun would rise again to bring back renewed life and wholeness. The Holocaust had taken away that right from five to six million Jews, but the grass, leaves, and flowers would grow again and the survivors would carry on.

The paratroopers remembered when tree stumps were covered with creosote so that the gliders could not land without catching on fire and kill all of the occupants. They recalled the outrage of cruelty, beyond belief that a Holocaust survivor

From Landsberg Liberators to the Eagles Nest

could be forced to watch her own child being burned to death. It was bad enough for paratroopers to see the destruction of homes, cities, and landscapes, but when the Allied forces came across that same mass destruction of human beings, the depiction of the Holocaust would always make them cry, or vomit, or doubt their own memory. How could it be that bad? How could people be that evil?

As C Company opened the gates to freedom, the displaced persons were let out into the strange country where they had been brought and forced into hard labor against their will. Because they had no home to return to, the prisoners still felt imprisoned among total strangers on the "outside." Some of them were too weak to leave the concentration camps. Women and children were found with swollen bodies and protruding abdomens. The survivors suffered from the cruelty of man-made forced famine and starvation. The skeleton-like bodies of grown men only weighed 60 pounds. What the paratroopers found was that some things are worse than death. In pity, the servicemen tried to give the freed prisoners anything or everything that they had in their pockets or packs. Even a piece of candy would express respect and sympathy, but the emaciated bodies rejected the kindness and it killed them. The thoughtful gesture gave prisoners peace in the grave that they were praying for.

Lest We Forget

Russ's injury in Bastogne kept him and others from going on to Landsberg concentration camp and the Berghof, but it was a relevant part of his 101st, 506, Co. C story that he said needed to be told and remembered. Their stories were shocking for Russ to hear, but provided him with a proud moment of respect and honor for his Band of Brothers who carried on and completed their history and rendezvous with destiny.

Many untold stories were buried deep in the minds of veterans memories or buried in unmarked Flanders Field graves where they died. Some bits and pieces of an account would slip into a moment of conversation at each of our Company C reunions. Those who saw it for themselves agreed that the Holocaust survivors were literally walking dead corpses ready to die and that was one of the topics rarely discussed. The few remaining, who did not die or were not injured, frequently chose not to talk about going on to the Berghof and Eagles Nest. How badly the servicemen would like to deny what they had seen. There would be such relief in their mind if it could be erased from their memory. Some almost did by not talking about it.

WWII veterans would like to believe that all the bodies laying around the battlefields and concentration camps were resting or sunning. Some tried to rationalize what they saw, attempted to diminish the reality, or wanted to believe that death is part of the cycle of life. It happens. Death is

From Landsberg Liberators to the Eagles Nest

inconsequential. It's to be expected. Each man had a choice to let go, become hardened by what they saw, or even try to excuse it or blame it on Hitler alone. At least they wouldn't have to suffer any longer or hold onto their last ray of hope. Just like what had been reported at other concentration camps, men of Company C could have buried all the bodies found at Landsberg in one mass grave like the German forces had done (sometimes while the prisoner was still alive). They could also try to spend the rest of their life trying to bury the memories of the war.

The importance of the Company C story is to talk about the emotional pain from what they saw, lest we forget the atrocities of war, and that they knew there was no excuse for mass murders. After the war had ended, it took thirty years before the 506, Company C paratroopers were ready to see each other again and start having annual reunions. The first one held was on America's Birthday, 1976. There were times when one of their men came to a reunion for the first time, hardly said a word and then when leaving stated firmly, "I cannot be reminded of our past. It was too painful and we will not return to another reunion. Take me off your roster."

Russ and his wife Rosemary went to an early reunion when it was in nearby Indianapolis, Indiana, but it was too difficult for her to be among an entire group of WWII survivors. Although she did

Lest We Forget

not know the details of Russ's nightmares, Rosemary felt that his screams were about the war. She may have wanted to protect Russ, thinking he was better off not hearing about or talking about the war. Neither of them knew how healing and supportive it was to be with his Band of Brothers and their wives. Everyone wanted life to be like it was before the war. After the reunion that year, Rosemary and Russ discussed the weekend and agreed not to return to another reunion, but Russ stayed in touch through occasional phone calls, Christmas cards, and he remained on the Company C mailing list.

The Berghof and Eagle's Nest

Even though there were not enough coffins to bury the bodies found in Landsberg, it was not the mind set of the 506 paratroopers to have another mass burial in one grave. When they found hundreds of dead bodies in the Kaufering complex, the US Army unit ordered the local townspeople to give a proper, respectful burial for each person.

From Landsberg, the Charlie 506 platoon was sent forward to Hitler's beautiful Berghof home in the Obersalzberg of the Austrian Alps. The small group was set back by the French 2nd Armored Division flow of soldiers returning down the crowded road with loot, primarily liquor from the tunnels and Hotel Platterhof. The 101st had ways of getting through and stopping them for their own

From Landsberg Liberators to the Eagles Nest

share of bottles. Once the road was finally cleared, the 3rd platoon set up headquarters for assigned guard duty.

The small group of Charlie men found cover for a place to set up their headquarters under one wing of the roof still standing in the bombed out shambles of the hotel. During bivouac their KP duty was made easier by finding a huge supply of hotel silverware, goblets, and trays. While staying in the ruined hotel, it was effortless and saved time to eat on what was available by simply throwing the found stash of kitchenware out the window after use, (saving their mess kits for later).

The Berghof and tunnel that led to the underground headquarters was secured by May 9, 1945, and guarded by the men of Company C. Part of the same 506, First Battalion who had duty at Hitler's Berchtesgaden hideout was to exercise the horses at Field Marshall Herman Goerings modernized 1000 acre medieval castle in Bruck, Austria. Bob Nelson and Ken Parker were taken by jeep for their first horse duty. Ken Parker said, "My first worry was that the massive (castle) gate was going to drop on us and stake us to the ground."

The two men recalled finding barrels of fine wine which they generously opened to fill their water canteens. At first, Ken was a bit hesitant with the obstinate horses because of his bad experiences at home with a large Tennessee walking horse that almost ruined his back, but the wine would help. "I

Lest We Forget

was looking for a small horse (preferably a Shetland pony)," he wrote for the January-February, 1994 Screaming Eagle Magazine.

The men also found resistance with a cabin of former displaced person prisoners. Not until Bob and Ken offered them some of the disguised wine in their water containers, did friendship break out. Bewildered, Ken Parker was finally getting back some confidence in his horse riding skills, but was met with a rude awakening that his calmer horse was unavailable to exercise. He was directed to mount another larger and stronger horse. Finally successful with the unfamiliar horse, Bob suggested with confidence that they should have a race.

The eyes of Ken's horse looked wild, the ears were pointed straight up, and it took off, intentionally leaving Bob well behind. When a farmer happened to pull a gate across the road the race horse was unstoppable as it easily leaped over and cleared the post. It headed toward roads, across fields, and when it saw poles that looked familiar they were no problem to the horse as it easily cleared each height. Ken had let go of the reins much earlier and was holding onto the horses neck for dear life. Ken Parker's fellow C company "buddies" had planned the whole thing. They knew the animal was a top jumping horse and had competed all over Europe!

From Landsberg Liberators to the Eagles Nest

When the First Battalion moved on up the mountain they were able to catch war criminals and Nuremberg defendants. The 506 occupied the town of Worth, Austria and established headquarters in Rauris, Austria. An Army Harley, like Russ had driven, was parked near the fluttering Stars and Stripes that had been raised on the flagpole in Berchtesgaden, Austria. Ten days after liberating Landsberg, Charley Company stood before the huge steel door that guarded the tunnel behind what had been the beloved, most beautiful, well known, but devastated remains of the Berghof.

Suddenly a trooper on guard heard the sounds of loose rock fragments, scraping metal, and then voices of German men, who claimed to be doing a survey of art treasures. They were denied entrance because they lacked a pass signed by Col. Robert F. Sink. The group of bare legged Bavarian civilians and high-sock lederhosen dressed men walked away as the Major cursed during an angry salute.

The scuffle sounds within the tunnel were three paratroopers who added to the stress on the guard who did not know they were there. The Charlie troopers emerged, excited with the finding of allowed legal prizes and keepsakes from the war. The nine hand-hammered silver framed cache of photographs of Adolph Hitler had been found and broken free from metal storage lockers within the tunnel.

Lest We Forget

Barter ensued with the paratroopers findings: a Nazi dagger, a Luftwaffe jacket, a German 88 shell box, and items they were permitted to ship back to the United States. Years later one of the photos from the cache sold for a mere $600.00 when a paratrooper needed the money more than he needed to look at that picture any longer. When the father of a Company C Colonel saw his sons picture of Hitler, he burned it to deface and destroy the painful memory of the war that his son had seen and gone through. One of the pictures was sold for $6,000.00.

Russ laughed, saying, "And all I got was a cut out piece of my parachute!" Then he looked lovingly over at me and said, "No. I have so much more. I have you."

Over recent years our family, friends, and students who have interviewed Russ have showed their interest and surprise that a remnant of his green silk parachute made it through the war, through three injuries, and in and out of four hospital stays. Russ kept cutting off a piece and giving it away until I said, "I have laminated one piece onto a page in your Currahee Book just to be sure you can't give it all away, but this is all you have left now. Let's save it for you to 'show and tell' when there is someone who wants to talk to you or meet you! That gives them a chance to hold a piece of WWII history in their hand."

From Landsberg Liberators to the Eagles Nest

I thought about what I had said and laughed, "Well, I guess they could do that just by shaking your hand! Russ, you really are a piece of history, an American treasure."

The Berghof oversize chalet had once been the center of the Third Reich where the entire invasion of Poland, France, and Russia had been organized. It framed the gathering of evil thoughts that conceived the concentration camps. It had once entertained distinguished guests including British Prime Minister Neville Chamberlain, the Duke and Duchess of Windsor, and Benito Mussolini, but Hitler hid in fear from the advancing 101st Airborne. After taking cyanide pills, he used his own service pistol to take the life of his beloved Eva Braun, and his treasured Alsatian/German Shepherd Blondi, before turning the gun on himself. The bombed out site was entirely destroyed, and during the 1950's the remains were completely removed. Today it is impossible to find the exact location, having returned to the natural landscape of the beautiful Austrian Alps.

The Berghof and Eagle's Nest became an important, proud part of Russ's story and what his Company achieved after the tragic loss of lives and injuries in Bastogne. Charlie Company went on, lest we forget, and completed their rendezvous with destiny until the war was over. They made it to the Berghof with hope and a ray of sunshine that would restore new life where flowers did bloom

Lest We Forget

again. The Eagle's Nest is a cozy restaurant that takes a strenuous hike to an elevator shaft deep within the mountain to get to. Tourists who still choose to venture there are able to see the remains of the structure much the way it was before and during the war. The restaurant boasts a 360 degree view high on top of the beautiful mountain peak.

    Charlie Company was left with a lot more than the keepsakes they brought home. They would always have the horrifying memories, injuries, and the lost lives of their buddies, but what meant the most was that they started without any history and now they leave a lasting historical memory, their rendezvous with destiny. The war came to an end with a very heavy cost and sacrifice for our freedom, but they were victorious. Lest we forget, the 101st will always remember and think of themselves landing and perched as Screaming Eagles high on top of an Austrian mountain, strongly in control of one particular Eagles Nest.

VI
"HOME ALIVE IN '45"

"When you go home, tell them of us and say, 'For your tomorrow, we gave today.'" — Unknown

21
A President's Death.
A Paratrooper's Marriage
— Russ Transferred to Tennessee Hospital

"Don't let the light go out.
Let it shine through our love and tears."
— *Peter, Paul, and Mary*

Above the familiar roar of two massive C-47 engines and suffering from his injuries, Russ clearly understood the announcement "President Franklin Roosevelt is dead." Although Russ was coming home in a Medical Transport plane from a Paris Hospital following his injury in Bastogne, he said, "I was immediately struck how unfortunate it was that Roosevelt did not live to see the end of the war. I felt sad for the entire country."

The plane began its descent for landing and refueling in Alaska. When the C-47 came to a stop, Russ realized how speechless the passengers were. Amid the silence there was incredible disbelief, while others started to ask questions. At the time there were no details of the President's death, April 12, 1945.

Before the age of television, President Roosevelt was able to maintain a strong image before the public who seldom saw him in a wheelchair because he insisted on being

Lest We Forget

photographed in an upright standing position without props and supports showing. There were a few citizens who did not know that he had polio. The Presidents unexpected, sudden death was caused by a massive cerebral hemorrhage.

White Sulphur Springs was bought by the Roosevelt's for a Polio Center and he had gone there for a rest. While sitting for Madame Shoumatoff to paint his portrait, he slumped over in the chair, almost instantly slipped into a coma, and died. At the funeral, Graham Jackson played "Going Home" on his accordion and then the congregation sang, "Nearer My God to Thee."

President Roosevelt had united and led the country through the most difficult depression period in our history and the mournful WWII battles massive loss of young American lives. The nation was caught mourning the death of their President while celebrating that servicemen were coming "Home Alive in '45."

The New York Victory Parade for America, January 12, 1946 was to celebrate Victory Europe, VE, and Victory Japan, VJ, days in honor of the servicemen who had done a magnificent job and would become known as the Greatest Generation. In the hearts of many, it was also the celebration for the life of President F. D. Roosevelt. The parade lasted for three hours, forty minutes as it proceeded down 5th Avenue.

A President's Death. A Paratrooper's Marriage

The following day newspaper headlines read, "Millions Cheer," and Gerald Evers of the 101st, Company C paratroopers participated. He remembered being given a white silk scarf made of parachute remnants to wear with the prominent sewn on 101st crest. Immediately following the parade, Gerry joined the participating GIs and went directly to trains leaving homeward bound for the deployment depot discharges across America. The war was over and units were deactivated.

Ultimately, Russ was not able to celebrate by riding in a ticker tape or home town parade because the war was not over for the hospitalized injured military troops. Russ was flown from Paris to Alaska and then Tennessee where he was admitted to St. Nicholas General Hospital. From his hospital bed, Russ heard the friendly voice of another young injured GI, speaking from the bed beside him. The man got up, looked for the name on the identification card and said, "Francis Russell Snell? My name is Harry Schwartz. We need to help each other out here. Are you ready to get well?"

From that introduction, a close friendship was born, grew, and lasted for over 60 years until Harry's death. During those years of friendship, Harry and Russ always called each other on their birthdays, many American holidays, and on Christmas.

Harry (Hans) Schwartz wrote beautiful poetry and was published in various magazines, including

Lest We Forget

the National Library of Poetry. An emotional verse that Harry wrote, reminds me of the moment he and Russ met:

> *"Life is full of sorrow,*
> *I search for a better tomorrow.*
> *I feel so much pain,*
> *Will I ever laugh again."*

Harry Schwartz had it on his bucket list to visit Russ again before he died. He flew to LAX and was met by his sister-in-law Miriam, who took him to rent a car. Early the next morning, Harry left her home to spend a week with us. At the age of 83, driving in a strange car through unfamiliar areas of Los Angeles freeways with holiday traffic to be exact, and making countless freeway exchanges was a very difficult, confusing day for him, but Harry was very independent, self-sufficient, and had determined that's what he wanted to do. Because he kept getting lost, it took Harry all day to get to our home the week before Christmas.

The most important thing to him was not for us to take him sightseeing. It was to spend time visiting, but there were a few places Harry decided he'd really like to go, including a day at what became his favorite place, the Palm Springs WWII Air Museum. He also wanted to go to one casino, but after just 15 minutes he walked over to us where we were waiting and said, "Alright, I'm ready to go." On the way to the car he said, "I just wanted

A President's Death. A Paratrooper's Marriage

to win enough money to pay for my airplane ticket and I did. Now I'm ready to go!"

One evening while sitting around the flickering lights on our decorated Christmas tree, Harry was proud to answer a few questions about the friendship he and Russ had enjoyed for so many years. It was Harry's chance to tell us some of his memories of the war and he said, "You know, Margie, that I met Russ in the hospital, right? He was so weak he could hardly eat and so I stood beside his bed and fed him. Russ was suffering from shell shock, the combat fatigue that caused complete physical exhaustion.

"One day I asked him, 'Russ, do you want to get well?' When he nodded that he did, I said, 'Then you have to get up and walk. You have to get your strength back.' He was so weak he could hardly stand and so I took him by the shoulders, helped him up, and let him lean on me. I held him up as we started to walk the halls of that hospital.

"It was very slow at first, we didn't go very far, and I would ask him, 'Russ, have you had enough? Are you too tired? Do you need to go back to bed?' He was determined to get well and would always say 'No. Keep going.' He was determined to get well."

One day I asked, "Harry, where are you from? You have an accent, other than just from New York!"

Lest We Forget

Harry and his wife Eva lived in the same apartment, downtown New York for 55 years and they were true New Yorkers. He said, "The happiest day of my life was when we bought a new car, but I was even happier when we sold it! Some days we'd drive around for two hours looking for a place to park or we'd have to park eight blocks away. We got along just fine all those years without having a car." That worried me because he was not use to doing much driving and he had just driven the rental car to come and see us.

Hans laughed and said, "You mean way, way back?! Where was I from? I came from Vienna, Austria, 1940. My parents were already here and so it was easy for me to get through. I was only about 19 and ended up volunteering for military service before I became a citizen."

Russ and I of course knew that Harry was Jewish, even though he respectfully sent us a beautiful religious Christmas Card every year. "If I may, Harry," I continued, "Could I ask you if you had any relatives in concentration camps?"

"Oh, yes, many. Most of them," he said without hesitation. "We never saw or heard from any of them again. It was like they never existed, but we had to go on. You can't look back in life and you can't be bitter. Bad, terrible things happen in everyone's life. People right around you are hurting, but they go on to make things better. I don't think about that now."

A President's Death. A Paratrooper's Marriage

Harry reached into his pocket and pulled out his wallet. He said, "I have something to show you that is a small, personal symbol, representing to me my appreciation and value for life, because I was one who was fortunate to survive the war." He found a very small velvet fabric bag and emptied the contents onto the table. Inside were two small jagged pieces of metal.

"When I met Russ in the Tennessee hospital following the war, I had to have surgery for these little pieces of flak shrapnel that was in my forehead." Harry pointed to his scar. "If they had gone a few degrees over, it would have caused blindness, or the Doctor said I could have lost my life. The surgery was successful and I recovered. That is why I decided to have value for life and not be angry. It does no good to be angry."

Harry and Russ celebrated life with small, lasting treasure reminders of being survivors of the war. They each kept the meaningful item of importance in their wallet and with them throughout their life: Harry's flak pieces that were embedded and cut out from under his skin and Russ's piece of camouflaged piece of silk, cut out of his parachute in Normandy were safely tucked away in their wallets.

I suggested, "Harry, you must have been proud and happy that you went back as an American and helped liberate the country of your birth. Thank you."

Lest We Forget

"Yes, but I didn't directly. I was mostly in Germany. At times I was a translator and would be going somewhere and hear someone say something in German so I'd respond and translate. They'd look at me wearing an American uniform, shocked that I spoke German."

When Harry was getting ready to leave, I wanted to fix him a lunch to take with him, on his way back to Los Angeles, for fear he'd get lost again. He had expressed his appreciation for his time with us and said, "No, I'll be fine," he insisted. "I just wanted to come and see that my helping Russ to walk again paid off. It worked, because he's still walking and now he's getting around better than I am!"

While gathering up the few things he brought, Harry told us, "All my life I kept a journal, but since the love of my life, Eva died I have not written on a single page. Now, I am going to go home and write about my visit with you. Russ, you and Margie have treated me so kindly. You fed me like a King and took me to places I'll never forget."

Harry Schwartz died shortly after visiting us, but we are forever grateful for his true friendship. The inspiration of his life was the gift that kept on giving. Harry really knew how to grow old gracefully and he is the one, in his youth, who got Russ up and walking again.

A New Castle Courier Times article, 1945, reported, "101st Airborne at Bastogne, Pfc Francis

A President's Death. A Paratrooper's Marriage

R. Snell, a paratrooper, was seriously wounded during the battle." Besides helping Russ to regain his strength and get well, Harry inspired Russ to truly appreciate the fact that he wanted to go HOME. He was ALIVE and at the age of 22, a "serious injury" would not make him a victim of the war.

Being blown out of a foxhole is a tremendous blow to the body, often accompanied with a severe concussion and loss of memory. Russ did recall that Rosemary Mitchell, the beautiful redhead that he broke up with before going off to war, came to Tennessee at some time. He thinks that she got on a train to go and visit him and perhaps to accompany him back home. Marriage was on their mind!

Although he broke up with Rosemary to keep her from worrying about him while he was in the war, there was no way to keep her from thinking about Russ or him from thinking about her. Because he did not want her to be home wondering if there was a bayonet pointed at his head or to find out that Russ as a 101st Airborne was on the front line of a battle, he tried to protect her from his pain. Russ did not want Rosemary to hear the news or wonder if he was one who died behind a hedgerow or blown out of a foxhole. Russ let her go because he knew there was a strong chance he would never see her again.

Lest We Forget

    Russ knew they could have gone on pretending and dreaming that everything would be alright when he went off to war. Young people tend to think that bad things happen to other people, but nothing wrong was going to happen to them. Russ would love to have had the tea leaves or fortune tellers foretell that he would not be one of the 77,000 deaths in Bastogne, that he would live, and that when he returned from war, he would have a woman waiting to marry and be his wife.

    It would have been nice if on the eve of Russ's departure to Camp Toombs airborne training there was a wedding with their friends and family. He would like to have gone through the war knowing that she was home praying for him and waiting for him to return "Home Alive in '45." That's what many servicemen did before they went off to war, but Russ did not want to be a hero because he was a paratrooper, and he did not want to leave a widow if he did not return. Russ was a happier soldier knowing that Rosemary would not be the one to receive his Dog Tag or medals if he died. But, in his mind he wanted to tell her to keep the home fires burning because he would be back to marry her.

    During the war, Russ enviously remembered the excitement when others were lucky enough to receive mail from a sweetheart or young wife back home. He recalled how lucky the others were to carry a photograph of a young bride or fiancee and

A President's Death. A Paratrooper's Marriage

all he saw was pin-up poster beauties of ladies he didn't know, but they reminded him of the pretty redhead he could not forget. When others shared stories about the loves of their lives, all Russ would think of was how painful it was to break up with Rosemary.

While Russ was fighting in the war, Rosemary was fighting a war of her own and finally did what Russ told her to do and thought she fell in love with Johnny, the city bus driver's son. It certainly did not take her long, however, to go back to Russ. Seventeen days after Russ was "Home Alive in '45," Francis Russell Snell and Rosemary Mitchell were married, April 29, 1945. They lived at her parents home for a short time until Russ could get a job and their own place to live.

Lest We Forget

F. Russell Snell is seen kneeling with his arm resting on his knee and behind him on their wedding day, April 29, 1945, left to right, his bride Rosemary Mitchell, brother Thomas Boliver Snell, Jr., and his wife Bertha Mae (Stevens). Shortly after their wedding in Rosemary's parents home, Russ and Rosemary had their first formal photograph taken together.

A President's Death. A Paratrooper's Marriage

The country was flooded with returning veterans who were looking for and needing a job. Women had become use to working and did not want to give up their jobs, but it was expected of them. The veterans who wisely saved their pay had an advantage over those who spent it. On their troop transport ship with 450 101st Airborne returning as a group, a paragraph in the Westerly News reported that the Dun and Bradstreet financial house, suggested the capital a veteran needed to start a business in a medium-size town (like New Castle) would need $2,500.00; grocery store, $3000.00; shoe store, $3,500; furniture, which Russ would have been interested in, would have been $7,500.00; and a small department store, the most, at $25,000.00.

Russ was not ready or strong enough to start a business and felt fortunate after a short period of time to get a job at Perfect Circle as a barometer reader for the temperature of steel used in automobile pistons. When the GI Bill opportunity was provided, Russ chose to use it to learn to fly. Jumping out of a perfectly good plane is not a natural act. While jumping into battle, there was something safer about gliding in a parachute than being in a glider or C-47, but during practice and training, next to Rosemary, the second love of Russ's life was flying. He decided that someday he would like to be a pilot and the GI Bill gave him that opportunity.

Lest We Forget

Russ loved the feeling, the view, and he wanted to share that passion with the lady he loved. Russ said, "I wanted to share the exhilarating feeling because it might be the closest to Heaven I'd ever get!"

One day, Russ called me over and asked, "Have you ever seen this? It's my Flight Record and Log Book."

The brown leather-looking heavy cover of the 3x6 inch booklet showed a lot of wear from heavy use. Some of the pages were folded in half to mark a particular spot. Russ address was 214 1/2 N. Tenth Street, New Castle, Indiana, phone 2, 590 Wx.

Each page in the log had a check list of 39 items, including the pre-flight procedures, taxiing, take-off, climbs, turns, stalls, spins, lazy eights, and around pylons. There were confidence maneuvers to evaluate reaction to emergencies, power landing, cross-country, making 360 degree and 180 degree approaches, and judgment state.

On one page an instructor had written a note and short comment that in the "Next flight, introduce 'Traffic Pattern' or 'Forced Landing,'" and it also stated, "Started on a Taylor Craft." After two months of training, there was a penned in note by the instructor simply stating, "Student suffers from airsickness." After all that time, it was surprising! Only mentioned in writing once, I thought of the possibility that Russ had a flashback to flying

A President's Death. A Paratrooper's Marriage

during the war and being shot at. Perhaps the instructor did not put it in writing because he wanted to protect Russ and help him achieve his goal to become a professional pilot. The effect of shell shock can last a lifetime. What matters was how Russ chose to deal with stress or airsickness, and how hard he worked at overcoming the struggles and effect of war.

After four months of training, a significant flight was from the little New Castle Airport, on to Winchester, and then to Muncie, which was about 25 miles from Hagerstown where Rosemary was born. On February 2, 1947, Russ flew his first solo flight to the Ruzicka Airport and Kokomo Municipal Airport. May 16, 1947, Russ finally reached his goal to share that heavenward exhilarated feeling and he wrote in his pilot log, "First Passenger. My wife."

The following week, May 25, 1947, Russ added another memorable event by writing in the log that one at a time he "Took Passengers Up. My Family!" It was on the third anniversary eve of D-Day that Russ wrote in another significant occasion, "Started Commercial. June 5, 1947." I drew Russ's attention to the interesting note and he commented, "Yes, my goal was to use my GI bill to become a commercial pilot, but my time limit to proceed ran out because Rosemary's dad, Leslie Mitchell, was furious and said, 'No you're not. My daughter is not going to be left a widow.'"

Lest We Forget

Russ happily became very successful when discovering he could sell anything! With a good job and lovely brick home, three and a half years after they were married, Russ and Rosemary had their first of two beautiful daughters, Jane and eight and a half years later Lisa Jo was born. But in between the birth of the two girls, something happened. Both Russ and Rosemary thought their happiness would be the same youthful excitement as it was before the war. They either didn't want to, couldn't, or had no experience how to talk and deal with the traumatic, emotional effect of war on their lives. They had mourned and grieved the loss of friends and family in different silent ways.

Right when the Great Depression was coming to an end, the war began. Women had to step up to fill in for the man's work at home and in the work place. Families were given Ration Stamps controlling how much meat, cheese and butter they were allowed. Only buying twelve ounces of sugar or three gallons of gas a week was a difficult adjustment. Tin cans were separated from the trash to be used for ammunition and battleships. Artistic posters appealed for bones to be saved and separated from the trash so they could be used in the manufacture of glue for airplane construction and in ammunition, but perhaps the greatest hardship was worrying about the life and well-being of all the servicemen. The unknown is often more difficult to live with than the facts.

A President's Death. A Paratrooper's Marriage

Russ fought back the odds of war to return to regular life, marry his bride and have a lifestyle that was a still small voice against tyranny. He had a beautiful family which took him as near back to the way life was suppose to be as possible. But one day Rosemary left Russ and went through court for a divorce. She may have rationalized that Russ was right. He told her to go on with her life when he left her to go off to war. That may have made it easier for her to leave him, because he left her. She felt the pain, struggles and aftermath of how the war affected Russ when he so frequently let out a frightening scream in the middle of the night. She did not know how to deal with being startled awake from a sound, peaceful sleep.

It was another shock in Russ's life. The war was over and now his marriage was over. He didn't know how to fight to save it because he had fought to end a war and didn't feel like fighting any more. Sometimes letting go is more powerful, but where should he go, what should he do? He turned to his dear friend Harry Schwartz.

Harry and his wife Eva took Russ into their tiny one bedroom New York city apartment. With a young son, it would be crowded until Junior went off to college. For 18 years, Harry and Eva pulled down the Murphy Bed to sleep in their front room, but because of their unselfish love for others, there was always room for one more when it was time to help a friend.

Lest We Forget

Harry took Russ by the shoulders as he had done before. He lifted Russ up and helped him walk again. Harry and Russ, the Screaming Eagle, went to the top of the Empire State building and Harry said, "Russ, you can still fly. Don't give up because you're a survivor."

Russ went home to Indiana because he had a good job waiting for him. He would never stop caring for the ones he loved. When Russ married and started a family he accepted the privilege and responsibility that he would always cherish. Love is a decision. Russ and Rosemary remarried because their relationship was not a commitment of duty or obligation, but love and devotion.

Best friends, F. Russell Snell and Harry Schwartz are shown visiting and looking at Russ's 1945 Currahee paratrooper album, 2004.

22
Rations, Crashes, and Blackouts
— Marjorie's Fears

*"Into each life some rain must fall.
Some days must be dark and dreary."*
— *Longfellow*

    A regular life during the war was not the way life was suppose to be because war has such a significant, profound impact on the home, but it helped my parents realize how many things we could get along without. My brothers and I were only allowed two pairs of shoes at a time. When our play shoes were too tight, worn out, and the war ration book allowed it, mom and dad bought us a new pair for dress-up and church. The church shoes were bought a size too large so that when they fit well, we could use them to play in for hide and seek, kick-the-can, or Ping Pong.

    Being frugal became a lifestyle that worked well in places where there were not a lot of shopping choices. We never thought of ourselves as being poor, but I knew we certainly had more than we needed. In comparison to what other children had in foreign countries, we seemed to have a few more toys, but probably not more clothes. That was good parenting. That taught me not to brag about the things I had. Our friends probably had more

Lest We Forget

clothes to go to school in. Because we were home schooled, we didn't need as many.

The toys and games we had were probably not actually more, but just different. Being Americans, our friends liked to see and play with things that their other friends didn't have. The things from the United States were usually ordered from the thick, wonderfully entertaining Sears and Roebuck or Montgomery Ward picture album catalogs.

While living in Texas and Arkansas during the war, our family was affected by restrictions on items that could only be bought with stamps from the use of our war ration books. When I was only two years old, I had my own books to be used for my needs. The instructions were very clear that "the book was the property of the U. S. Government, and Office of Price Administration. Punishment for abuse of its use ranges as high as ten years imprisonment or $10,000.00 fine or both." The book was non-transferable and only to be used on behalf of the person to whom it was issued and in the event of departure from the United States, the book had to be surrendered from use. Canned goods, baby food, and children shoes were limited.

There was also a salvage program and I remember how carefully my parents saved the requested items. Having uncles in the Navy, Air Corps, Marines, and two who worked in the Boeing Consolidated Aircraft of San Diego led us to be very

Rations, Crashes, and Blackouts

appreciative of their contributions to our country. During WWII Boeing was manufacturing the B-24 Liberator, our most produced, and the B-17, the most rugged bombers. A salvage program that mom and dad followed and taught my brothers and I to help with included saving paper products so that they could be recycled to print our newspapers. Food cans could be used for supplies our uncles might need in manufacturing supplies at their work or in the war. Everyone was also very frugal with some habits acquired during the depression that continued during the war. Our tea-drinking aunts hung their tea bags in the cellar to be reused. My parents rule was to turn lights off every time we left a room and the habit continued.

We were just like most WWII children, not feeling poor at all. It seemed very smart and clever that mother could remove a dress or shirt collar, turn it over, and sew it back on. During the war a new fad started, to sew leather patches on a worn out shirt or jacket elbow. Who knew whether it was to cover a hole or to look stylish!

Sometimes I wore cardboard or a piece of tire rubber inside my shoes when the sole was worn through. Being a real Tomboy who loved playing all sports, riding my bicycle, and racing, I wore my shoes out faster than I should have. Everyone came up with some pretty clever, ingenious ways to save money. We were only allowed to take the amount of food we intended to eat. Waste not, want not.

Lest We Forget

My parents believed that the war would soon be over and they wanted to go overseas again. We were about to board another train and visit our grandparents and California family, but this time from the station near our home in Little Rock, Arkansas. Mom and dad enjoyed traveling the train, without the responsibility of driving and following a map, which meant trying to figure out on their own, the most direct route. There was no MapQuest or OnStar back then and gas was still being strictly rationed.

"Meet Me in St. Louis," was a popular song with significance to dad because his parents moved there from Buffalo, New York where he was born. "Chug, chug, chug went the motor," and there was that other song:

> "Chug, chug, chug! The engines going;
> Ding, ding, dong. The bell rings too;
> Toot, toot, toot! The engine whistles,
> 'Clear the track I'm coming through.'"

My favorite locomotive story was that my grandfather Edgar Delafield was an engineer on the train that went to the Kimberly Diamond Mines in South Africa, but my favorite memory was of a family vacation while living in British Guiana, 1952. We boarded a train to travel the rails through tropical villages of that country. Watching people of various nationalities and customs was very

Rations, Crashes, and Blackouts

educational to us as well as to those of the country, as they watched us!

Dad was always a very friendly extrovert without a bashful bone in his body, and would speak to everyone who walked down the narrow aisle. He had just learned a new mathematical riddle that he told at least a hundred times! Although it's been more than sixty years ago, I can still hear dad saying, "Do you have a moment? I wonder if you can figure this out for me?

"There were three traveling salesmen who stopped and checked into a hotel room. It cost $30.00 and so each man had to pay $10.00. Later, the owner and manager decided and said, 'That's really over-charging them. The room should only be $25.00.'

"He gave the young Bell Boy $5.00 to return to the three men. The boy took the money, but while going to the room he was trying to figure out how to evenly and fairly return $5.00 to three men. He didn't want to make anyone angry, so he decided to give each man a dollar back, costing them $9.00 each instead of $10.00. The Bell Boy tipped himself and pocketed the other $2.00.

"3x$9.00=$27.00; Plus the Bell Boy's $2.00=$29.00. What happened to the other $1.00?"

Dad could string the passengers along for hours, chuckling at himself, with his familiar giggle, for puzzling his subject. It entertained all of us for a while, but eventually we took time to play some

Lest We Forget

card games and enjoy looking out the train window at the scenery. We could still hear Dad in the background, every time another victim came along!

Those were better moments, happy memories without the fear of war. Hopes were rising that better times were ahead of us during the war as well. We were on "The Little Rock Express," for another three day trip to visit our family in California, but this time Dad was with us and I had a new baby brother. Hardin Tyne Delafield was born January 1, 1945, the first baby of the year in Little Rock, Arkansas.

The customary flood of gifts for the first newborn of the year had been discontinued because of the war. My parents still felt blessed because a doctor's family in the church had a little boy less than a year old and they passed on everything their baby had outgrown to Hardy.

A few months later, another member of the church pulled Mom and Dad aside, crying and pleading that she had to talk to them. "I'm so concerned about our family. My husband has been leaving for a week at a time during the last few months and he won't tell me where he's going. I believe he's being unfaithful to me." Her problem was the opposite of my parents and their friends who were both enjoying the happiness a new baby brings into the home.

The continuous, monotonous clickety-clack of the track rhythmically rocking across the steel

Rations, Crashes, and Blackouts

rails was enough to put us to sleep. Even mother, with dad aboard, had a better chance of getting some sleep. Everyone was a little more at ease, knowing that America and the Allied Troops were having more success. For that reason, my parents could accept the invitation to work in Panama.

Because gas and tires were still being rationed, families were afraid to travel very far in their cars. We were going to visit our families and so the train was the best option. While traveling through Arizona, my parents heard rumors that the war in Europe was over. At every train stop, dad tried without success to buy a newspaper. We finally arrived in Los Angeles, after traveling across heavily crowded railroad crossings and hearing all the honking horns. The train windows were all lowered and everyone was looking out.

Our locomotive was heavily loaded with servicemen fulfilling their war duty assignments. Traffic stopped at the crossing signs, where swinging familiar lights were blinking to the clanging sound and warning of our approaching train.

Car horns were blowing and people were waving to the young men in uniform, yelling, "The war's over. The war is over!"

Every American citizen and our military servicemen knew that we were in it to win it, but one of the servicemen yelled back, "Who won?!"

Lest We Forget

As the train passengers were laughing and crying with emotion, the answer could be heard above the cheering proud crowd, "We did!"

Trains across America were bringing the troops "Home Alive in '45."

My parents home in Little Rock, Arkansas was sold and we were preparing to move to Panama. We moved out of the country right about the time Russ came home from the war. A few months were spent in preparation to leave our homeland and time to be with our family because we would be gone for four years. The 1940s was a time in America's history when we were very patriotic, especially in San Diego where everyone could see aircraft carriers out in the harbor, the Coronado peninsula, and frequently see the airships from nearby Miramar Marine Corps Air Station.

On the 4th of July, 1946, there was a large air show planned at the San Diego County Fair. Dad's sister Thomasea, her husband Paul, children Paul, David Tallant and our family went there for the day. That was my first memory of any State or County Fair. Over 30,000 people spread out through the rows of food booths and prize winning sheep, pigs, and cattle. There were beautiful ribbons for the best peaches and delicious pies, but when it was time to watch the air show, everyone went and gathered in the bleachers, along the fence, or on top of their cars and truck beds in the parking lot.

Rations, Crashes, and Blackouts

The show narrator spoke over the loud-speakers to describe the various practice and techniques during the aerial display for proud, enthusiastic spectators. The otherwise very happy day ended in shock and sadness as the crowd screamed in disbelief when two of the planes rolled into each other and collided in the air. There was also a military plane whose pilot had just been married the day before and promised his young bride that he would give up his flying career after this final assignment. The plane approached from high above us and the crowd expected it to round off in front of us and head back skyward toward the heavens. Before thousands of people the nose dove straight into the ground and exploded into a fiery, flaming, smoking disaster.

As a frightened six-year-old, how well I remember the changing mood of the crowd. Everyone was leaving. The happy atmosphere was over and it seemed to take forever to get out of the parking lot.

Living in Panama after the war, 1946-1950, was a little like being in Honolulu, before the war because of all the U. S. Military services stationed there. The thing to do on weekend nights was to go to our post office box and hopefully find mail from our family back home. We frequently met up with some other Americans, the Whitney family, who had children the same ages as Trevor and I. Their daughter, Ann, became one of my friends. We would

Lest We Forget

go into Panama City and walk the streets, which were bustling shoulder-to-shoulder with sailors stationed on the Canal Zone. I was just a little girl walking along, eating an ice cream cone, but I was looking at the sailors. That's when I first fell in love with men in uniform! They reminded me of my uncles whom we had been taught to respect and be very proud of. The sailors wore stiffly pressed white bell bottom trousers, a high stand up "choker" collar, completed with white shoes and the familiar white "Dixie cup" cap to complete their smart uniforms.

As we walked along the sidewalk, Ann asked me, "Do you know what a pregnant lady looks like? That's when she's going to have a baby."

It wasn't something I had rally talked about at the age of six or seven, but she drew my attention to it when she said, "Let's count how many we can see with a big fat belly."

The war was over and servicemen everywhere were ready to settle down and get back to the American home way of living. They wanted to get married and start a family and many brought their sweetheart or young wives over from the mainland to live with them in family housing. Because we were Americans, we could go shopping at the Military Commissary.

For a while we lived in an American Military office building that had been converted into our home. We loved the design because when we came

Rations, Crashes, and Blackouts

in the front door it opened into a long hallway clear to the far back of the house. We could close all the doors, kick and throw balls as hard as we wanted to because there was nothing in the narrow hall that could get broken.

That Panama home was on a Military Compound where some officers still resided. Directly across from us, the Cockles lived with their two sons, Dale and Bobbie. We felt like the luckiest children in all the world when their dad brought home some military supplies for us to play with. We had a high quality walkie-talkie crank phone that we used from their home across to ours. Each of us had our own little pack of rations, first aid kits, and a set of army utensils that clamped shut for traveling.

Once a week the DDT truck drove up the small dead end side road where we lived to spray for malaria mosquitoes and we ran to hide in the smoke, imagining the spray was from exploding bombs and falling buildings. None of the adults knew of the danger to our health.

Yes, the war was over and there was a lot of joy and celebration, but there was still a lot of uneasiness. After I was sent off to bed I could hear my parents talking together or visiting with friends about the war. Discussing the atomic bomb was not something they talked about around their children, but I found out that the lady in Little Rock, Arkansas who thought her husband Raymond

253

Lest We Forget

(undisclosed) was being unfaithful to her was actually a nuclear physicist working for the Government and had been working on the top secret Atomic Bomb.

During the war, it wasn't safe to turn lights on at night for fear plane bombers could attack the Canal Zone like they attacked Pearl Harbor. To continue awareness and preparedness, the alarming air raid horns came on during occasional unannounced times and even as children we knew to turn off the lights and go to the wash room. We turned on the opaque blackout light bulb. The low 25-watt black bulb allowed just enough light through the orange or dark yellow circle at the bottom for us to move around if necessary until the all clear signal was heard.

The Whitneys had not moved in yet, but their side of our duplex home was still empty when we moved to the isthmus. One morning mother loaded our little brother, Hardy, into the back of the car and rushed over to pick up Trevor and me from our piano lesson because she had a load of wash running in our new, now vintage Maytag Wringer Washer washing machine. When mom arrived we jumped into the car and started begging her to take us over to watch dad and the crew take down the big three-pole canvas tent.

"Please, Mom. Please. Can we go see Dad?" That was a big deal and something kids don't get a chance to watch very often, and so mother agreed

Rations, Crashes, and Blackouts

with the understanding we could not get out of the car because she was in a hurry. Unfortunately when we got there the tent was already down and so we did not stay.

As we approached the street where we lived, we could see people running and we heard sirens of police cars and fire trucks. The road was already being blocked, so we could not drive through. Mom quickly parked when she saw a spot and threw Hardy on her hip and started to run. She instructed Trevor and I, "Hold each others hand and stay right beside me."

While running we heard people yelling about a plane crash. When we were stopped, mother told the policeman, "I need to get through, because that's right where we live and there is a lady in our home expecting me right back. I have to get through."

We were led through the crowd and as we arrived back home we could see the tail end of a plane embedded into the concrete in front of our house. The smoke and smell was frightening and we could see a wing protruding through the roof of our duplex home. The little Panamanian lady was so frightened that she ran across the yard and with her adrenalin strength, jumped a six foot high cement wall. Shortly after we got home she returned and was still shaking with fear.

"Mrs. Delafield, it was horrible. It was so loud. Everything shook and I'm so glad you're back

Lest We Forget

home safely. I was worried about you and the kids. Where's your husband?"

An American single-seat military fighter plane started to have engine trouble and the pilot realized he was in danger. He aimed the plane out over the ocean and bailed out, but the plane veered and returned overland, crashing directly in front of our home. While living in Colon, Ann, Bobbie, Trevor and I played in the back yard together and we found metal from the plane, embedded into the ground and so we use to dig looking for pieces. We went along the sidewalk and found pieces there as well. Trevor kept a bullet that exploded on impact and felt that was his symbol of living through what could have been injuries or death to our family at the time. We felt it was providential that we had not come directly home from piano lesson and our car was not at that corner or we were not playing in the yard when the military plane crashed in front of our house.

While we were still in Panama we received a telegram that Uncle Paul Tallant was killed in a small private Piper Cub Plane. It happened near their home with his family, my cousins Paul and David, watching. Uncle Paul was a tall, handsome young man who took advantage of opportunities to live life to its fullest. He was adventurous in his love for nature which led him to becoming an excellent photographer. Paul learned to fly with his friend Buzz Templin, but one day when their family stood

Rations, Crashes, and Blackouts

watching from an open field, the plane was unable to pull up properly from a dive.

Fears can conquer us, or we can conquer them. My cousins Paul and David both became pilots. Russ learned to fly even though his C-47 took on heavy flak attacks during the war and he lost friends who died in plane crashes. Russ said to me, "I want you to know what it feels like to jump in a parachute." He didn't know that his invitation helped me get over my fear of heights by going up in parachute rides at Knotts Berry Farm and the San Diego Wild Animal Park!

My fear of flying was overcome by the need to fly, but to this day, I always stop what I'm doing when an airplane flies over lower than I expect. It eased my mind when my sons moved away from the direct path of large military planes flying out of the Riverside Reserve Air Base at the Van Buren exit off of Highway 215, near the National Cemetery.

As a child, I was trusting and confident in the security of home, but children always have experiences, fears and images that raise an alarm or cause them to question their safety. Shortly after seeing the air show plane crashes, we flew to Panama in a large, lumbering DC-3. The massive 63 foot long airship with "C" in its name stood for Commercial, but the planes were actually converted C-47s like Russ had flown and jumped from for two combat battles. Another "C" was that Russ was in Company C, Charlie Company who nick-named the

Lest We Forget

C-47, "Cheeky Charley," as well as "Gooney Birds," but I also became his other "Gooney Bird!"

Of the 16,000 built, there were still many C-47s in use on the 70th Anniversary celebrating the end of WWII. When my family flew, 1946, in the DC-3 to Panama, I thought 21 passengers were a lot of people, but today, there are 300 or more passengers in most long distance flights. The pilots of the C-47 claimed it was the greatest airplane of all time, but it was the 101st Airborne paratroopers from the "Greatest Generation" of all time who made it famous.

VII
LIVING LEGACY OF A GREATEST GENERATION PARATROOPER

"The past has a fascination that if hidden crumbles into obscurity."
-Unknown

23
From Languish and Loss to Love Again
— Russ Was Down but Never Out

"Soldier rest! Thy warfare o'er,
Sleep the sleep that knows no breaking,
Dream of battled fields no more,
Days of danger, nights of waking."
— *Sir Walter Scott*

How could a loyal basketball-loving Hoosier like Russ, end up in California? He was born, grew up, married, and except for his time in the war, had worked most of his life in the small town of New Castle, Indiana. One day he made the decision and simply said, "We're moving! We're going to California."

It was in the back of Russ's mind for some time because he and Rosemary had already sold their beautiful Indiana brick home and moved into a little bungalow apartment. It was decorated to fit the cozy little space and style that Rosemary loved. Now that their girls had moved away, they no longer needed a large home. Keith and Lisa Hindsley had been working in Denmark when Lisa came down with severe Rheumatoid Arthritis and had to come home. It worked out well to have an immediate place to move into, because the Hindsley's took the

Lest We Forget

little apartment over the garage where Russ and Rosemary lived.

Jane and Dave Wood were working in Brea, California. Before very long Keith got a job in Southern California, providing an opportunity for them to move out West and be close to Lisa's sister. Russ thought that's where they should be as well, but it was not easy for Rosemary. All her lifelong best friends from the Hagerstown and New Castle neighborhoods, schools, churches and work were her constant companions. Rosemary kept thinking and dreaming that someday her girls and family would come back home.

One day while reading their hometown New Castle Courier Times paper, Russ clipped out a small paragraph that said, "Riverside, California is the fastest growing city with the most job opportunities in the United States." He slipped the news clip into his wallet and decided that's where they were going. He had talked about it long enough. That would bring their immediate family back together with reassurance he could easily get another job.

Having been in the furniture business so long as owner of his own store and top salesman in others, he had no doubt or fear that it was the right thing to do. Russ's confidence, knowing he could jump out of a perfectly good airplane as a paratrooper, was the same self assurance he had

From Languish and Loss to Love Again

that he could take another flying leap and move clear across the United States!

Without any fear or hesitancy, Russ's unwavering resolution helped Rosemary to believe in the decision and she started to pack their belongings. He thought by promising her all new furniture and accessories when they got to California, it would be something exciting for her to look forward to. It was a bonus working in furniture stores because he had first chance at holiday discounts and sales. With the additional employee discount, Russ could usually figure on a 70% discount.

When my parents retired, that's what Russ did for them: they sold all their furniture in Idaho and moved to Riverside, but it was easier for them because they had moved all their life and had to leave their furniture behind. Furniture was nothing they ever got attached to, except Mother's first piece of furniture, her little cedar chest. Cora took it with them everywhere they moved for 70 years. Russ was able to get all of my parents coordinated furniture to fill their retirement home at 75% discount!

If Russ and Rosemary sold all their Indiana furniture it would save the cost of paying a moving van to take used furniture clear across the country. Russ knew he could buy all new furnishings when he got a job, but it was not that easy for Rosemary. Her furniture had also come from "good deals" she

Lest We Forget

had selected out of Russ's store in New Castle. Taking a little bit of Indiana with her was so important that Russ agreed to transport it if that would make her happy. Rosemary already felt displaced by leaving her friends and Russ decided it was not fair to uproot her from the things in her home that she was so comfortable with. He called the New Castle Allied Vans furniture movers to schedule the Snell's move to California.

When they arrived in Riverside, Rosemary wasn't ready to buy a home. Russ found a lovely apartment complex in Canyon Crest that had a lot of green belts and trees with some seasonal changing colors, reminding them of Autumn in Indiana. While waiting for their furniture to arrive, Russ and Rosemary went to Desert Crest Country Club, Desert Hot Springs, to rest and relax following the long cross-country drive to California.

The Snell's spent several years vacationing there after their daughters moved to California. Their son-in-law Dave Wood introduced them to his father Gayle who had a retirement property in the Coachella Valley. His brothers Loren and Harold Wood were also original owners of Desert Crest Erickson properties and gave the Snell's such a warm desert welcome during cold Indiana winters. It was a place Russ and Rosemary learned to love. With golf, four different temperature hot mineral water pools, jacuzzi, an exercise room, spa and indoor shuffle-board courts, they knew there would

From Languish and Loss to Love Again

be constant visitors while they were waiting for their furniture to arrive.

During the wait, Russ decided to drive around and look for furniture stores where he might like to work. He drove out to Indio and just for the fun of it, went in and talked to the manager who immediately offered him a job! Russ laughed, "Now wait a minute! Thank you, but I just arrived from Indiana and I want to look around a bit!"

Riverside was just an hour away and so they drove into town, stopped by their recently acquired apartment, and went into a few furniture stores near the area. Russ said he liked the looks of one in particular. Inside Krause's Sofa Factory, Russ was especially impressed with their beautiful show room, the sales people were very friendly, and so he decided to ask if they were hiring. Russ was given an application which he filled out and handed back to the manager. She asked him to stay for an interview. With all the experience and success in Russ's background, she hired him immediately. "Could you start on Monday?" she asked.

Russ smiled appreciatively, but said, "I'd be happy to accept your offer, but I'm on vacation. We'll be moving in next week and I'll start one month from today!"

They smiled, shook hands in agreement, and Russ went back to tell Rosemary the good news so that she could relax. Russ knew she had confidence

Lest We Forget

in him as a businessman, salesman, and that having a job would make her happy.

The family came out to celebrate, help them unpack, and get comfortably settled in a new, enjoyable routine. They would again be living close enough to have frequent opportunities for family togetherness. Unfortunately, the joy was short lived when Rosemary was rushed to the hospital with a massive heart attack, less than a year after they arrived. As soon as she was stable enough, the family was called together by Doctor Donald Williams who informed them that Rosemary would not survive without having a quadruple bypass as soon as possible. They were made aware of the details and seriousness of the procedure following the recent infarction. It took a great deal more than a medical decision. It would require the support and agreement of the family who could already see her weakened condition, but after praying together Russ signed the consent.

Almost beyond belief, the family was called together again after the surgery and told the graveness that she was faced with next. Rosemary was a diabetic and the surgery had worsened the unstable vitals. The respiratory complications and diabetic instability put her life at risk again. The Doctor informed them that she was developing gangrene from poor circulation and that she would not survive without an amputation of her leg, but he did not believe she would survive the surgery.

From Languish and Loss to Love Again

Dr. Williams asked, "I have to ask you the most difficult question for any family to have to answer. Do you want me to do everything humanly possible to prolong her life, knowing she has no chance of living through the surgery, or do you want to be with her and spend time together while she is alive?"

The girls mother and Russ's wife of forty years was already on the respirator to keep her alive. Whatever decision they made, how could they ever find peace to know if they made the right decision? All they were able to do was respect the Doctor's opinion and trust in God's compassion and mercy. After struggling to make the right decision, they came together in agreement and Rosemary was taken off of the respirator. There would be no second surgery.

Rosemary died April 2, 1987 at the relatively, much too young age of sixty and she was buried in a very patriotic ceremony at the Riverside National Cemetery on Van Buren Avenue, April 7, 1987. The three WWII battles that Russ fought in rewarded him the Purple Heart and two Oak Leaf Clusters for injuries that almost cost him his life. There were three battles that Rosemary fought that did cost her life. Her major heart attack required a coronary bypass, the diabetes a recommended amputation, and the shortness of breath led to her death with respiratory insufficiency.

Lest We Forget

Russ was physically and emotionally exhausted because he continued to work full time during Rosemary's four months of hospitalization. With such love, devotion, and commitment, Russ drove to the hospital every morning for a few hours before going to work and again after work to spend a few more hours together before driving home. When the sun came up, his alarm clock rang after a few hours of sleep and he repeated the process all over again the next day.

The share of cost expense for medical intensive care had almost taken the Snell's entire retirement savings. Homes cost a lot less in Indiana than in California and it was necessary for Russ to return to work a few days after the funeral, but he ended up in the emergency room. Russ was admitted to the intensive care unit with bilateral-double pneumonia. His family was still grieving and had not yet recovered from the loss of their mother and grandmother, when the doctors told the family Russ was critically ill. The family was faced with the shocking possibility that they might lose their dad as well.

Russ was finally discharged from the Riverside Community Hospital intensive care unit in a seriously weakened condition, but he focused on getting well. Just as he had recovered from his injury in Bastogne by walking the hallways of the hospital in Tennessee, he was told it would require weeks of rest, eating healthy, and gradually

From Languish and Loss to Love Again

increasing his walking exercise to get his strength back. Russ leaned on Harry Schwartz when recovering from the WWII battle and he leaned on his daughter Jane, their hospitality and good cooking to get Russ well again. Dave, Jane Wood, and their four children, lived on a golf course in Brea, California and while everyone was at work, or school, Russ walked the golf cart paths. He increased the length of time walking until he was strong enough to return to his home and work in Riverside.

Russ had just returned to work when I went to Krause's Sofa Factory to purchase a small, inexpensive sofa. The cost of my home and having college-age children, Rob, Rick, and Tanya, demanded being very frugal and working overtime on weekends. In order to make the sale, Russ offered me an additional discount on the sale price, so I accepted the offer!

While walking to the desk to fill out the paperwork, Russ commented, "I noticed you're wearing a nurse's uniform and I just want to thank you. I have great appreciation for nurses because this is my first day back to work after my wife died following complications from surgery. I just got out of the hospital following my recovery from bilateral pneumonia. I guess I almost died too. Thank you for your service as a nurse."

It was obvious that Russ was very sincere in expressing his deep appreciation. Apparently, I

269

Lest We Forget

responded as a nurse by giving him a little support and reassurance. I didn't remember what I said, but Russ said he did! You said something like, "It's not easy to go through the loss of a spouse and the work of recovery after your own illness. It's understandable, as I know some of the difficulty of feeling alone and working hard, but you're doing the right thing and not letting it stop you from getting back to work and going ahead with your life. Good for you!"

When Russ finished writing up my purchase order, I wrote a check and a note with my son Rick's name, because he had a truck and would be the one to pick up the furniture. Russ transferred my note from the form with my phone number and stuck it in his wallet. It remained there for six months.

One day his assistant manager said, "Russ, for Heaven's sake call her. There's only two things that can happen. She'll either say 'Yes,' or 'No.'"

That evening Russ got on the phone, hung up a few times, but finally got the courage to call me. "Hello. Is that Marjorie?"

"Yes."

"You probably don't remember me, but I'm the sales person who you bought the small sofa from."

It was time to give Russ a little support and reassurance again and so I said, "Yes, of course, I remember."

From Languish and Loss to Love Again

"I was wondering if you would like to go out to dinner with me?"

That's not what I expected. I thought he wanted to tell me about another sale, but what made the phone call and question so interesting was the timing of it. Just the previous Saturday night, when I noticed that Rob had not been out with his college friends three weekends in a row, I went up to talk to him.

"You're home again," I observed. "Why aren't you out with your friends?"

Unselfishly, Rob replied, "I just don't feel right about going out and having a good time when you're home alone."

"Rob, I want you to know that it's my job to take care of you kids and not your job to take care of me! Go to the phone, call some of your friends and get out of here! OK?"

That made me realize I had to keep my word, take responsibility for myself, and go forward with my life (just like I told Russ to do). The next time I was invited out with friends or on a date, I would accept the invitation to show the kids I was alright. It was Russ who called!

If Russ had called any sooner than he did on that particular night, I would have turned him down. He claims I intentionally went to Krause's to buy a "Love Seat," but I correct him and say, "No, I didn't. You insisted on it. You gave me a discount so I would buy a 'Love Seat.'"

Lest We Forget

How we met is a favorite memory in our "Love Story," because when we got married, Russ ordered ten yards of the same beautiful ecru and sky blue tapestry for me to make a matching bedspread and drapes to go with the "Love Seat."

During our developing friendship, one of the first things Russ and I did was to make it very clear to the other that we had no intention of remarrying. That made it easier on both of us. After we became good friends Russ told me one day, "Remember when I called and asked if you remembered me and I invited you to go to dinner with me? Well, I was so afraid to ask you that I had already gone ahead and made a reservation so I wouldn't back out from calling you!"

I started to laugh, "I'm not laughing at you because you were afraid, but because that night, the first time I went to dinner with you I got so scared and I was afraid. When you called it sounded casual and not very threatening and so I felt safe in that way, but..."

Russ interrupted, "You were afraid?"

"Your phone call didn't feel that romantic, but the evening was. You even ordered an impressive "Flaming Cherry Jubilee!"

Russ smiled, "It was a long time since I dated and I wanted to do it right. I didn't know how to invite you out and so when I made the reservation I ordered the dessert ahead of time too, but you were scared? Why?"

From Languish and Loss to Love Again

"When you got out of the car to come and open the door for me, I saw you reach into the side pocket on the door and I thought you might have pulled out a knife. We were at the Cliffhanger Restaurant on the way up to Lake Arrowhead where there was a beautiful view. It was a clear night and we could see all the lights of San Bernardino and Riverside in the distance. After dinner you wanted me to walk over to the wall and enjoy the beautiful view of flickering city lights. I think there was only one other car in the parking lot so I kept my eyes on you very carefully. Nothing happened, but when we got back into the car, I kept my hand on the door handle.

"I didn't relax until you started up the car and said, 'I should have told you. When we got here I put my Swiss knife in my pocket with my fist around it, because if you have to hit someone and there is something firm in your hand, it gives a much stronger blow. While we were looking at the view, I was going to make sure nothing happened to you.'"

Our friendship continued to grow, but when we started to talk about "What if we got married," the discussion always led to the difference in our age. Knowing that our friends and family were concerned about that as well, it wasn't difficult to see that Russ was torn with his own mixed feelings. I felt like sometimes he was trying to say we should

Lest We Forget

not get married and sometimes he was trying to convince me (or himself) we should!

One day Russ said to me, "My daughters are married, but your children aren't and they are still in school. If we ever decide to get married, I want you to know that I would never want you to feel that I was coming between you and your kids. Your family will be equal in importance as mine are to me."

I knew that my daughter, Tanya, believed that because she thoughtfully said to me one day, "Russ has really been like a father to me."

Our relationship reminded me of a favorite scripture story in Ruth, "Don't tell me to leave you or not to see you, because where you go, I'm going to go. Where you live, I'm willing to live. Your family will also be mine and your God is mine. Where you die, I will be buried too." (Ruth 1:16)

Russ's concern for my safety, protecting me with his knife, and unselfishness of my time with my children was something money cannot buy. When a woman is treated with that kind of respect, a man gets more in return than he could ever hope for. I knew that Russ would cherish and honor me and I knew that I would love him back with all my heart. We were married on Russ's birthday, September 21, 1989, a private family wedding in the San Bernardino historic church next to the romantic Victorian Edwards Mansion where we had a full course, sit down formal dinner.

From Languish and Loss to Love Again

Without my realizing it at the time, Russ loves living in the desert, but I certainly did not want to live there. I knew not to get married thinking I'd change him! When we did get married, Russ kept the home he bought at Desert Crest Country Club because we had a large home in Canyon Crest, Riverside. When we both retired, the decision where to live was made by putting both homes up for sale. He thought it would be healthier to live in the desert with all the ways to exercise and keep active. I was sure a home in a retirement community would sell quickly, but the four bedroom home sold in three days with a three week cash escrow! Quite reluctantly for me, we moved to our full time home in the desert!

A concern of mine was when I thought about Rosemary being buried at the military National Cemetery in Riverside and I wasn't sure how the family would feel about Russ wanting me to be buried there too someday. Russ reassured me and the family by saying, "It's alright because I just happened to be married to two good women. Rosemary would be happy that I have a good wife."

When neither of us were working any longer, we started looking for new interests to keep us busy. Russ had no problem because he had golf! He knew I had always wanted to learn to paint and become an artist so he insisted that I start taking art classes and join the Spa City Paletteers Art Club. We joined the Palm Springs WWII Air

Lest We Forget

Museum in order to be involved with the history of his military past.

Before we were married, Russ thoughtfully wanted to prepare me for something that he did not think should be a surprise after our marriage. He said, "I need to let you know that because of being in the war, I still have bad dreams sometimes. If I wake up screaming, just grab my arm, wake me up, and I'll be alright."

Over the years, well-meaning family and friends frequently gave Russ WWII videos and books for his birthday or Christmas presents to show their appreciation for his service. He was often asked if he had returned to Normandy following the war, especially for the 50th or 70th Anniversary of D-Day or the end of the war.

Russ had little interest in reading the books, DVDs, and old video sets. They remained unopened in the tightly sealed cellophane wrap. He would simply say to me, "been there, done that," and I could tell he did not want to be reminded, but over the years he came to the realization that students need to know the history. The schools teach very little about WWII.

"Why has everyone bought me movies and books about the war?" Russ was perplexed, but did not want to sound unappreciative. One day when he came back from playing golf he said, "Now they're all insisting I go to see 'Saving Private Ryan,'"

From Languish and Loss to Love Again

A docent at the Palm Springs WWII Air Museum told Russ and me that he went onto a school bus to be the tour guide. The student teacher introduced him and said, "This gentleman, will be your escort. As he talks to you, he will tell you about World War Eleven." The teacher did not know how to read Roman numerals or that there had only been two World Wars and so Russ knew he needed to tell his story. But, he knew it would be very painful to talk about.

The well-intended gifts to Russ were expressions of thoughtfulness trying to express everyone understood, but no one truly understands war without being there. Six months after the movie came out, Russ was trying to be casual about it and said to me, "Some of my golf buddies have seen 'Saving Private Ryan' and they keep asking me if it is realistic. I think now that we can rent it, I'm ready to see it. I will only watch it if we can see it together in our own home, but I just want it to be the two of us."

I reassured him, "OK. We'll pick up a copy for the weekend."

Saturday evening right after dinner, Russ and I decided to sit in our recliner chairs, get comfortable, and watch the movie together. Before very long, as the production progressed and became more emotional, I gasped at some events and looked over at Russ. I thought he had tears in his eyes and so I said, "Honey, why don't you move

Lest We Forget

over to the sofa with me?" I got up and moved to the warmth of the big white leather sofa. Apparently he was glad to join me, because he came right over and sat beside me.

After a short time we were holding hands. Trying to hide my tears and be strong for him, I leaned my head on his shoulder in appreciation, but I knew we were crying together. Speechless throughout and after the movie was over, we just sat there for a few moments. Russ broke the silence and with a shaky voice said, "It could not have been more realistic. That's the way it was."

"I didn't know," I hesitated. "Did you notice," I continued while struggling for the right words, amidst my tears. "Did you know the movie was based on the 101st, 506? More surprising, it was Company C, Charlie Company. It was really as though it was about you and your specific company Band of Brothers." After pausing, I realized Russ was still in deep thought. I added, "And, it was about two brothers. Were you imagining that could have been you and Tom? The actor was a Tom. Tom Hanks. There were just too many emotional connections. It's no wonder you said, 'That's the way it was.'"

The rest of our evening was very emotional. I knew it was especially sensitive for Russ, because I couldn't get the movie off of my mind. Russ had kicked his shoes off, trying to relax. Not until 10:30, after trying to watch the news and thinking about

From Languish and Loss to Love Again

going to bed, did I realize how emotionally compelling and forceful the story was to him.

Again Russ came over and sat beside me. "I think I'll tell you something." With a trembling voice and a long pause, he continued, "I've never told anyone this before," and he broke down and cried. I gave him as warm and understanding a hug as possible without knowing what he was going to say, "You're OK, Dear. Take your time. It's OK."

"Remember when I told you before we were married that if I let out a scream at night, just grab me. Shake me. Wake me up and then I'll be alright? Well, you woke me up so many times over the years."

There was another long hesitation as though he didn't know if he wanted to tell me. He must have also been thinking and wondering how to tell me. Russ thought that by waiting until we went to bed, it would be easier, but he found out it wasn't. After sobbing together, he was able to continue. I listened carefully to understand his trembling voice, "Every time I yell, it's the same thing. All these years it has been the same thing. It is exactly what really happened in Normandy, over and over, and over again." I listened to Russ as he tearfully let out the pain of an over 65 year old memory that was too painful to tell anyone before.

"After fighting in battle all day with buddies dying all around me, I made it to the top of a mound where an 88mm was firing down on us and

Lest We Forget

men were falling beside me. There it was, the machine that was mowing us down, but we got him and I can still see right in front of me, a German officer with his head blown off and hanging by the skin from his shoulder. I see it again every time I scream."

We could hardly stop crying together. Russ was able to tell me what he had hidden and held inside for over 65 years. That image was suppressed from talking about except for being released during his subconscious screams in the middle of the night. During the coming month it was very apparent to me as a nurse that instead of being awakened in my sleep with his startled flailing arms and horrendous yell, the shriek was occurring less often. Then it was back. After reaching for him, I patted his chest to calm him and he fell right back to sleep, but I couldn't.

The next morning I said, trying to be sensitive, tender and yet with determination in my voice, "Do you remember yelling again last night?"

For years we didn't talk about it. We had been married and lived with it for twenty years. Sometimes he'd say, "I had another bad dream again last night, didn't I? I'm sorry."

Sometimes I'd say, "Do you remember me waking you up last night?" It went on like that, always wondering, suggesting, thinking and my occasionally asking, "Do you remember what you were dreaming last night?"

From Languish and Loss to Love Again

Russ always answered, "Oh, I don't know. I'm fine."

...and dandy, I thought. A government postcard was sent to Thomas Boliver Snell when being notified of his son's injury during the Normandy battle. Russ was being discharged from the hospital and going back to his company. He wrote on the corner of the card, "I'm fine and dandy, so please don't worry about me." Besides the physical injury, there was an emotional injury that he fought with during the rest of WWII, throughout his life, and he didn't want me or anyone to worry about him.

"You haven't had one of those bad dreams for a long time," I continued and reminded him. "I think it helped when you told me what your dream was about."

"I do too," he interrupted and recognized.

"Last night it came back though, and I'd like you to see a doctor. Tell him what you've gone through for all these years. It's been sixty-five years, dear. I'll call the VA today. okay?" I thought it was time to see if Russ could be helped.

"Well," Russ hesitated, "I'll be alright.," but he could tell by the expression on my face I was serious. "If you think that's necessary. OK, whatever you say."

Russ and I had to wait several weeks for the referral to be approved and scheduled, giving us a lot of time to think and for me to make mental

Lest We Forget

notes of what Russ's dreams had been like. We also kept thinking about the "Saving Private Ryan" story we had watched together.

At the 506, Company C reunion, October 2, 1998, Moline, Illinois, the hosts featured a "Saving Private Ryan," movie poster that director Steven Spielberg had signed and written on with his appreciation for their service. It was sent to our group for the opening of the movie, but it pales in significance and importance to the intimate time Russ and I had together after watching the movie in the privacy of our own home.

The memories of times that Russ's dreams woke me up were important because I wanted to be able to tell the doctor about his nightmares if I was asked for details. One time Russ knocked a lamp off the night stand and onto the floor. Many times he'd yell and say something I couldn't understand. Once he yelled, "Get down," and I wondered if he was trying to protect me. He never told me that occasionally he'd talk in his sleep, but I learned that he did.

The months wait was over and I looked at the calendar for the time of our appointment. Funny thing, but at that moment I remembered one of Russ's dreams. It was shortly after we were married, newlyweds in our first home together.

Russ's mumbling voice woke me up one night, but it was clear enough for me to understand, "Cutest little pussy."

From Languish and Loss to Love Again

Shocked, because Russ never swore, used slang, or spoke disrespectfully. I answered him, "What did you say?"

"The cutest little pussy."

"Russ, what in the world?"

"Have you ever seen a Cat on a Hot Tin Roof?" he continued.

I broke out laughing so hard that it woke him up. If I had been around other people, I would have been blushing as red as a radish. At first I wasn't sure if he had been teasing or sleeping. My laughing got louder. When he tried to find out what I was laughing about, he started laughing at me, not even knowing why I was laughing so uncontrollably. It would have been nice to have awakened him like a soft purring kitten!

"Please, tell me what's so funny?" he asked amidst our hilarity.

Finally, I was able to tell him the entire conversation and we started laughing all over again. I was laughing so hard that I was crying and I grabbed my stomach in pain. "Stop," I yelled, "We're going to wake the neighbors up and they'll wonder what's going on over here."

"That's great," Russ laughed, "Let them think that!"

A couple of days later we went to the VA to talk to the Doctor, but I didn't tell him that particular memory. Russ has asked me why not!

283

Lest We Forget

If Russ could take his rifle apart and put it back together again with his eyes closed, I should not have been surprised that he would talk in his sleep, because they could all talk and walk in their sleep. I've been told paratroopers kept going for so many hours that they could all march and fight in open-eyed slumber.

While visiting with our friends, Bob and Alice Morales, about his experiences in WWII, he said, "I had four brothers and all of us wanted to do our part. A recruitment officer said to me, 'No. You have to be at least 5'4" and you're only 5' 2" tall.' I started screaming and yelled at him, 'I don't care. I'm going.' The Navy broke down just for me! 'Alright,' he said, 'Get over there.' They put me in and I was a Net Tender."

"I know what that is!" I said to Bob. "I think that's on an aircraft carrier when there are those nets around the deck to keep anything from falling into the water. When I was seven or eight years old in Panama, right after the war, we were allowed to get on a big carrier going through the Panama Canal. Most of the deck hung over the land of the docks, but the area where we had probably just come through the locks, I believe the ship was level with the ocean. It took so long to get through with a huge carrier that we were able to get aboard and be taken on a tour of the ship.

"The sailor was the son of one of my parents friends from Little Rock, Arkansas. They contacted

From Languish and Loss to Love Again

mom and dad and gave them permission to visit their son. As we were walking around the deck, I remember the handsome young man in his sharply starched uniform say to me, 'Marjorie, are you afraid of the water?'

"Of course I wanted to be brave and strong like my military servicemen uncles and said, 'No, I'm not scared.'

"He took me by my arms and swung me out over the net and let me down. I could clearly see the big huge ocean below me. He confidently knew that I was safe, but I was a petrified little girl who would never let anyone know it."

"No, that's not a Net Tender," Bob smiled. "I was the man tending and laying the anti-submarine nets and booms down, protecting the waters. I was in rough, critical conditions, protecting the coasts of Guam, the Philippines, Solomon Islands, and Guadalcanal.

"I remember very clearly the times of a loudspeakers cry, 'overboard, man overboard,' but I also remember some good times. Young guys have a sense of humor and one day I wasn't sure I heard right, 'dog overboard, dog overboard.'

"I guessed the man's name or nickname could have been 'Dawg!' Nevertheless, we went into full rescue mode, just like we were trained to do for any man. I'll never forget the cheers and yells of all the men when we saw that little dogs wet wagging tail come aboard!"

Lest We Forget

No man, or dog left behind! The dog was their mascot, being cared for by one of the men on the Navy ship, and was definitely worth saving. If any American is in danger, everything will be done until that life in peril is brought back to safety (even if it's a dog). Maybe Russ was having a WWII nightmare after all when he said in his sleep, "Have you ever seen a Cat on a Hot Tin Roof?" Perhaps it was a home in flames with a hot tin roof during one of his combat battles. A cats life should be worth saving just as much as a man, or his dog!

On the day for Russ's appointment, December 11, 2008, at the Loma Linda VA Hospital, it seemed like hours waiting in the office to see the doctor, but it had only been 15 minutes when Russ's name was called. There was the usual greeting, "Mr. Snell? Your wife, I assume? I am Doctor Schroeder. And, what are you here for today, Sir?"

We had all shaken hands respectfully and Russ answered, "Well, I'm here because my wife thought I should talk to you."

The Doctor looked at me, back to Russ, and said, "Why don't you just go ahead and tell me what's going on?"

Russ started out with a comfortable, short response, "I was a 101st Airborne paratrooper in WWII, and I guess I went through some pretty hard times."

From Languish and Loss to Love Again

As Russ paused, the Doctor asked, "and? Were you injured?"

"Yes," Russ replied, going on with a way to briefly describe his experience, "I jumped on D-Day; Zon, Holland; and went by truck to Bastogne, Battle of the Bulge. I had injuries in all three battles."

The physician looked up attentively and with increased interest replied, "I guess you did. Can you describe it or tell me any details?"

Russ didn't answer. He just looked over at me. I was use to that. In Russ's interviews at a few schools and even with our families questions, he'd look at me or hesitate. Because I wanted to make it easier for him, I'd answer or try to fill in what I thought was significant and important, but difficult for him to talk about. Dr. Schroeder waited and so did I, because he had not asked me.

"Has it been difficult for you to talk about over the years?"

"Yes, pretty much. Guess I just didn't want to talk about it," Russ laughed and pointed at me, "until this little lady came along!"

"Maybe I can reassure you that you're not alone."

When Russ smiled, but still did not reply, the Doctor said, "Would you like your wife to tell me? But, I want you to fill in and respond. Add to what your wife says or even correct her or disagree with what she says. Alright?"

Lest We Forget

To me, the doctors comment was obvious, because he didn't know us yet or why we were there. How were we getting along? Was there neglect, lack of support, or even elder abuse? As a nurse, I started telling Russ's story concisely and as professionally descriptive as possible. A doctor's time is valuable and I didn't know how much of it we would be given. The important things needed to be said before we left, and I was very nervous. I told of Russ's experiences and some of what he had gone through and concluded, "The most important reason we are here is because he has had nightmares ever since the war. He was brought home following his wounds in Bastogne and taken to a hospital in Tennessee. The doctors told him, 'Just go home. You'll get over it.'"

Doctor Schroeder interrupted me, "Did they actually tell him that?" Russ shook his head that they had.

"Yes. They discharged him and sent him 'Back Home Again to Indiana,'" I smiled. "Russ took their advice to the best of his ability and went to his hometown of New Castle, Indiana. While still in the hospital he contacted his former girl friend and within a month they were married, but Russ was not alright. He doesn't remember for sure, but he thinks he may have been readmitted to the hospital for a while. The newspaper said that Russ was seriously injured in the Battle of the Bulge. I assume he was dehydrated, starving, and in shell

From Languish and Loss to Love Again

shock so he needed time to get his strength back. I recently found out that the worst emotional injury happened in Normandy, but he went on after the wounds of each following battle, back into the hospital, and right back to his unit when they thought he was able."

Talking to physicians did not usually intimidate me, but it did that day. When I'm nervous my mouth gets so dry I have trouble swallowing and of course that makes it difficult to talk. Maybe that's one reason I was very sympathetic to Russ not wanting to talk about the war he lived through and wanted to put behind him, like the doctors told him to do.

To me, it seemed like I would have been pretty arrogant, controlling, and out of place to tell Russ he had a problem and needed to see a doctor. After all, he had raised a wonderful family, at one time owned his own furniture store, and been a successful businessman. When I met Russ he was manager of the Riverside, California, Krause's Sofa Factory. He had about ten months of certificates of merit and a couple additional for best Salesman of the year. While still in Indiana, Russ won a trip to Europe for he and his wife Rosemary as top salesman for McGrady's Furniture Store, New Castle, Indiana.

My patriotism, belief in, and love for Russ, along with the doctors definite interest in what Russ had experienced, helped put me at ease. As

Lest We Forget

confidently as possible, I "reported," to the Doctor what I would have said if I was his office nurse. "When we got married, 1989, and were comfortably settled, Russ pulled out a small metal combination locked box from the file cabinet. While dialing, he told me the simple four numbers to unlock the contents in case I ever wanted to put anything else in the secret container."

For 20 years I had worked well in close medical partnerships and proximity with the physicians during medical crisis and cardiac arrest of intensive care patients. Psychiatry was a comfortable area for me to deal with the emotional needs of patients and their family during intensive care, because I had experience as head nurse in the psychiatric clinic of White Memorial Hospital, Los Angeles. I had my highest score on the California State Board in psychology, but that day, speaking on Russ's behalf, I was afraid to do the talking and felt intimidated because I thought the doctor would wonder what took me so long? With my knowledge and experience as a nurse, I should have brought Russ in sooner. I should have, but rationalized, I didn't think Russ would have gone or been willing to tell a doctor what he had lived with for all those years.

I told the doctor, "Russ said to me one day, 'I have something that might interest you. I don't want us to have any secrets and so you need to know about this and I want you to know the

From Languish and Loss to Love Again

combination numbers of this metal file.' From inside the container, he showed me his WWII medals that had lodged there ever since the war.

"It's difficult to surprise Russ and so he was very excited to open his present on our first Christmas. He had no idea that I had taken his medals and had them impressively displayed on a royal blue velvet background in a shadow box frame to show-case and exhibit them. The non-faded ribbons were beautiful because they had not been exposed to light for all those years.

"Russ was very pleased to see them hanging so proudly behind glass. I said, 'You earned these medals and they need to be out to share with friends and family.'"

Continuing the conversation, I tried to concisely articulate to the doctor how Russ warned me of his dreams, didn't want to talk about the war, and how he acted during some of those nightmares. I explained what happened when Russ and I watched "Saving Private Ryan" together. I told the doctor exactly what Russ saw in his nightmare when he woke up screaming. The story actually brought tears to the doctor's eyes and he was in no hurry for us to leave. Doctor Schroeder wanted to know about each battle and where Russ was hospitalized.

Dr. Schroeder stood, turned to shake Russ's hand, and said, "Thank you, Sir, for your service and sacrifice for our country."

Lest We Forget

We were asked more details about Russ's service, not medically but in the interest of history. Russ said, "I made it and came "Home alive, in '45."

While the doctor and Russ were talking, I leaned over to pick up a folder that was leaning against my purse. It was on the floor, out of sight, but available in case I thought it was appropriate to show the doctor. I handed him the copies I had made of some of Russ's records and two photographs I had placed beside each other on a scrapbook page. "I think that because a picture is worth a thousand words, these pictures before and after the war are professional portraits that really show the effect of war. The first one shows the sparkle in Russ's eyes and passion to serve his country. The other one is right after the war, probably in Tennessee, when he was discharged from the hospital. The style of the formal portraits are the same, but the one before the war is without his medals on his uniform and the other with some of them after the war. There's a striking difference in the first photograph where he has a big smile, but in the second photograph his eyes say it all. The sparkle is gone, showing his fatigue and stress."

Doctor Schroeder looked at the pictures and carefully analyzed the expressions on Russ's face before handing them back to me, but I commented, "You may keep them if you'd like. They're copies I made for you."

From Languish and Loss to Love Again

Left: F. Russell Snell, August, 1942, is shown shortly after entering the 101st Airborne Paratrooper Training. With joy, sparkle in his eyes, and pride in the 101st airborne, he begins service for his country.

Right: Russ is shown, April, 1945, "Home Alive in '45," but with weight loss and the strain of war. His eyes were speaking for him, "I wasn't dead, but I wasn't fully alive either." During the days of seeing more dead bodies than living people, there's a part of you that dies with them.

The doctor was very touched and appreciative of Russ's story. He simply stood up again and walked around his desk where Russ and I were sitting. As we stood, he broke his silence as he approached us and said, "I'd like to thank both

Lest We Forget

of you." His outstretched arms pulled us toward him. As we stood shoulder to shoulder, the three of us cried together emotionally. He gave Russ another strong, man to man handshake, "Thank you again, Sir. I will always treasure your story."

Doctor Schroeder picked up the papers again as he sat back down at his desk and said, "Mr. Snell, it has been a real pleasure and privilege to meet a 101st Airborne paratrooper and now I'm going to be able to help you, but I think just telling your story to your wife and again to me today has already helped you a lot."

Russ acknowledged that it had and the doctor told him, "I am going to write an order for a low dose of a medication to keep you from having those dreams so often. It may not take them away completely, but perhaps more significantly with the diagnosis of post traumatic stress disorder, your military pension will be increased. Although you will not receive, but deserve back pay for the past 65 years, beginning today your pension check will be enough to make a difference from now on. It is not what you earned and deserve, but I hope it will make you realize that your country appreciates your sacrifice and what you did for us."

We didn't expect that or ask for any favor, and we certainly didn't know what to say. Finally Russ shook his head and with that beautiful, big smile said, "You sure made my day!"

From Languish and Loss to Love Again

The doctor added, "I've seen thousands of patients suffering from the effect of war and there is a lot of fighting between couples who have such lack of trust or respect for each other. I also see marriages with such strong feelings of anger and resentment because they became victims of the war and it affected their general health. It is a privilege to spend time with both of you today. Mr. Snell, you gave me so much hope and belief in the greatness of our military and American citizens who have good values and love for their country."

There's a strangeness in dreams. Nightmares, bad dreams, shocking and stressful experiences can often be turned into a source of humor and pleasantness if we so choose! Russ's war nightmare brought us a refreshing glimmer of hope and togetherness. Russ was tenacious, denied despair and fought against depression by becoming optimistic. He had enduring love to take the place of adversity, and turned that hope into love for others. That's how Russ told himself life was good, because he was alive. Of course it wasn't always the good life. Many nights it was a literal living nightmare. Many days were spent full of nervousness and confusion, but as long as there was an ounce of life in him, Russ felt like he was in good shape compared to his buddies who were dead.

As if questioning the date of Russ's own birthday and how old he was, whenever asked how long he was in the service, Russ could quickly,

Lest We Forget

always answer, "Two years, eleven months, eight days." During that period he narrowly escaped death countless times and saw indescribable suffering and loss of lives. Every time the enemy killed one from Charlie Company, Russ felt like they killed a part of him. It would have been easier to die than to watch the death of his own, because you're left to die their death over and over again for the rest of your life.

Worse than seeing newsreels portraying the war or movies creating images of battle, Russ had been hearing it, seeing it, reliving it in his sleep for 70 years. The sound of bombs whistling past his ears, the constant explosions of 88mm anti-tank, anti-aircraft artillery, flak guns, and the crashing of blown up buildings will never be erased from Russ's mind. Because it is beyond belief, that was reason enough to bury the story in his mind and not talk about it for so long.

It's human nature not to remember the bad things unless it is so bad that it is vividly engrained in our subconscious forever. Without dealing with life's bad memories and tragedies, they will resurface, until dealt with through medical intervention, medication, counseling, therapy, or making a conscious decision not to be victimized. Accepting that he could not change the past, but he could change how he responded to the past, Russ was able to live a productive, successful life and be a positive person. He is the best example that there

From Languish and Loss to Love Again

is hope for those suffering from post traumatic stress and the tragedies of war.

Animal lovers know how keenly aware pets hear things. When visiting our children, their pets Buddy, Kip, and Rasta were already at the door because they heard the family cars coming up the driveway long before we did. Animals can sense an earthquake and sit up startled long before a person feels the rumble. Imagine the effect of war noises on the farm animals, family pet, and citizens. In perspective, those of us who have not experienced the sounds of war need to imagine what our servicemen went through. God knows war is hell. Why don't we? Each of us should be as open-minded and willing to listen to the earth shaking sounds of war as startled animals are who don't know what an earthquake is.

The crash of shrapnel was like a room full of disorganized Lambeg snare drummers playing the loudest drum in the world. When I thought about what the paratroopers heard, I understood better why Russ said he could not wait for his chance to jump out of his C-47 before it exploded. The sounds of war caused permanent loss of hearing, requiring Russ to wear hearing aids in both ears.

It was impossible to prepare or train the servicemen and civilians how to handle the shock, sounds, and stress of war. The gardens and markets were taken over by the Nazi Germans. Even a beautiful day could not be appreciated or

Lest We Forget

enjoyed for constant fear of being bombed and face imminent death. For five war years, life was spent in sleepless nights and hungry days. There was nothing to be thankful for except to be alive.

Paratroopers were well-trained in strength and courage for battle, but it had to also be applied to handling emotional and physical pain, shock, and death. The horrors of war were brought so close that they could smell, touch, and hear it, but they didn't have time to show any fear through fatigue, being nervous, depressed, or incapacitated with a splitting headache and certainly not laugh like some people seem to do under stress.

Russ wondered when the war was over if it was the end or an opportunity for a new beginning and he chose to make a clean start and not dwell on what he had gone through. Over the years, when Russ is asked a question about the war he often says, "I don't remember," but there has never been a day in his life that he didn't have at least one thought about being in the war. There were days and nights with details Russ could never forget and wish he could. During Russ's occasional returning nightmares years after he had been treated for post traumatic stress disorder, he believes that life itself is a good dream and not a nightmare. We would always choose to make the best out of life.

When we left Dr. Schroeder's office and were walking to the car at the Loma Linda, VA Hospital, Russ spoke of the doctor he saw in the Tennessee

From Languish and Loss to Love Again

hospital, 1945. "When I was discharged the doctor told me I'd get over it. He didn't know I never would, but he was right about one thing. I needed to be told that in order to do something with my life, I should do something for others. He said in order to achieve my future goals in life, I needed to not look back and go forward with an optimistic future. Get a life, and I did."

That philosophy led Russ into becoming a faithful, long-standing member and officer of Optimist International. Whenever difficult circumstance arose throughout his life, he could quote by memory the phrase that was appropriate. He lived his life with Christian values and the Optimist Creed by promising himself "To be so strong that nothing can disturb your peace of mind. To be too large for worry, too noble for anger, too strong for fear, and too happy to permit the presence of trouble."

We drove down the road where we used to see an old handmade sign that had been there for years. It had probably been painted by a lifelong farmer when he realized the developers were starting to remove the orange groves and farmland of surrounding properties. That corner became the entrance to Loma Linda and San Bernardino's Hospitality Lane with rows of their finest restaurants. Each structure represented the fulfillment in someone's life of a soaring high dream for the future.

Lest We Forget

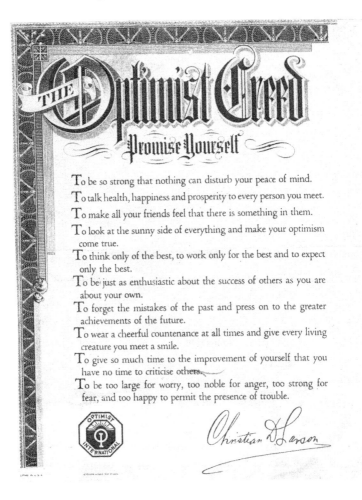

F. Russell Snell kept the original, yellowed with age Optimist Creed document, as shown, in the file with his most important papers. It was memorized word for word, became an important part of who he was, and how he lived under every circumstance of his life.

From Languish and Loss to Love Again

The sign was beginning to fall over in the open field of overgrown weeds where the large, flimsy, roughly painted words said, "Hold onto dreams, for if dreams die, life is a broken-winged bird that cannot fly."

24
Faith, Family, and Future Generations
— Russ and Marjorie's Retirement

"It is foolish and wrong to mourn the men who died. Rather, we should thank God that such men lived."

— *General George S. Patton Jr.*

The war did come to an end, but too many people died and they could never be brought back. The only way to keep them alive was to preserve their history by telling their story for future generations. The Charlie Company reunions also came to an end at an emotional 2006 gathering of the last surviving eight paratroopers from their unit.

Washington D.C., 2006, was the emotional, patriotic location chosen for the aging paratroopers and their families to meet. On the last day of our reunion, we visited the recently opened WWII Memorial and walked around the almost sacred grounds of the Memorial and Arlington Cemetery.

The tour bus door opened for us to proceed to the 101st Airborne Memorial just outside the gate of the Arlington Cemetery. Major Jan Kenneth Gleiman, awaited our arrival from the WWII Memorial and looked poignant standing beside a large red, and white carnation wreath with a beautiful royal blue satin 101st, 506, Company C

Lest We Forget

banner. He stood strong and impressive in his uniform and matching beret.

While unloading the buses of elderly paratroopers, we gathered together as a family around the 101st Airborne Memorial. Russ and I walked forward to read the famous D-Day marble engraved quotations by General Dwight Eisenhower and Prime Minister Winston Churchill. With canes, wheel chairs, and walkers beside them, the eight remaining Company C veterans sat down on the provided folding chairs directly in front of the memorial built in their honor. Following introductions, Major Gleiman respectfully referred to the location as a "sacred site," adding that he did "not feel adequate to the task of thanking the men of the 101st Division, and C Company in particular. We truly owe our liberty to those heroes. But for me it is personal."

He continued with excerpts of an emotional story that many of us had recently heard the details of. "My father, a young medical student during WWII, was born and raised in Slovakia, (which became) a tiny puppet state within the Third Reich, that tried to avoid the upheaval of war and Nazi avarice through capitulation and cooperation. Not an honorable existence for a proud people.

"My father was conscripted into the Slovak militia, a ragtag military unit for the purpose of conducting hard labor and eventually to be used as an expendable force in a last ditch effort against the

Faith, Family, and Future Generations

Americans. (He) endured the separation from family and friends, the pangs of intense hunger, the ravages of illness, the wanton neglect of the Nazis, and the devastating carnage of Allied bombings. My father lived in fear until his liberation at the hands of Charlie Company. At that time he was hiding with an Austrian farmer. My father had a limited ability to speak English and this proved to be a saving grace as he was summoned to translate for Captain Al Hassenzahl," (who was sitting among the eight men).

Major Jan Gleiman spoke to us as having been a young infantry lieutenant stationed near the Demilitarized Zone in Korea. Ironic de ja vu, he became an officer of the 101st with A Company of the 506 Infantry. His personal interest came about because his battalion commander compelled him to search the legacy of the 506.

Young Gleiman said, "I learned about the exploits of the Screaming Eagles in Normandy during the D-Day invasion. As I delved into their sacrifices and bravery during Operation Market Garden, and as I reveled in their tenacity during the Battle of Bastogne, my admiration for the men of the 101st grew by leaps and bounds, these men who did the impossible in the darkest of times. I felt my father would regale me with tales about a crack group of battle hardened warriors, the epitome of fighting men. They were that and more, but my father said instead, 'They were some of the kindest

Lest We Forget

men I ever met. They approached us refugees and defeated soldiers with no malice or bravado, they were genuinely concerned for our welfare.'"

Jan Gleiman's life was influenced by the extraordinary painful life his father had endured as a displaced person in a small Bad Hall Camp. The Senior Gleiman told his son and wrote in his memoirs of marching as a hard labor military where he saw the horrors of bombardment and nerve-shattering frequent alarms and air raids. He recalled waking to the sight of two big pots, one with herbal tea, the other on a long wooden table with pieces of unusual bread. It was known as "brick bread," made of "rye flour, mixed with potatoes, dry beans and dry peas in the form of a brick." On one occasion the residents were met with a friendly group who had come for some provisions and provided them with some brick bread. Embedded and hidden inside was a "friendly secret" of some bullets and small guns.

On one occasion a large, powerful German lady manager passed out small green bricks of soap so that they could finally have a warm shower, shave, and chance to wash their underwear. The soap was imprinted RIF, which later the German woman explained meant, "Rein Judishes Fell, pure Jewish fat." Many literally became sick and would never use the soap again. Lubomir wrote, "To this day I shutter at the thought the soap might be the legacy of the people we once had known. Much

Faith, Family, and Future Generations

later in my life, I thought often about Stalin's cynical remark that the death of one person is murder, the deaths of millions simply statistics."

While gathering around the 101st Airborne Memorial, the afternoon became dark and gloomy. The unbelievable stories continued to be told, lest we forget the reason for the sacrifices made in WWII. While translating for the 506, Company C, Lubomir Gleiman and Gerry Evers became close friends. Continuing to work and help maintain the camp for some of the multitudes of displaced persons, the facility was finally closed, and Lubomir realized he faced an uncertain future. "Refugee in a foreign country, penniless and separated from his family," without a country or home to return to because it became occupied by the Soviet Army, Lugo was "distraught and in the depths of darkness when a simple act of kindness dispelled his gloom."

Lt. Gerry Evers wrote and signed a simple paper. Major Jan Gleiman said, "For the next three years as my father searched for his family and tried to reestablish his life, (he) would use that letter to establish rapport and find work, go back to school at the University in Innsbruck, and eventually he would use the letter in his family application for imigration to Canada and later the United States."

Major Jan Kenneth Gleiman's father Lobomir Gleiman was anxious to attend the 506, Company C reunion, but passed away May 5, 2006 just five months before we met in Washington D.C. For fifty

Lest We Forget

years the nearly worn through simple note from Dr. Gerry Evers had been folded into eight sections to fit a pocket or wallet where it remained close to his heart, a symbol of what brought him to freedom. Also translated into German, it simply said, "Lobomir Gleiman was employed from the 14th of May, 1945 till 25th of June. Gleiman was moved to a farm in the community of Rauris, Austria." G. H. Evers, 1st Lt. Int Prch Co-C, 506.

When the younger Gleiman found himself an officer in the same group which his father had been involved with and was speaking to the Charlie Company men at their reunion 61 years after the war, there was not a dry eye among us. He concluded by saying, "This unit and its fallen heroes will forever be remembered for their bravery and sacrifice. I believe that is not enough for our remembrance to be complete. We must also remember their love, their humanity, their goodness and their morality. While they were soldiers ready to fight and kill, they were also good men who through it all, believed in the fundamental worth of all human beings."

The gray sky had produced a heavy mist that turned into a light rainfall. The wife of one of the 506 paratroopers leaned over to me, where all the wives were standing physically and emotionally behind their men, and said, "Marge, the rain is as if God's tears are falling from heaven above. He is

Faith, Family, and Future Generations

grieving with us, for all who have died ahead of our men."

Major Jan Gleiman closed by saying, 'I ask you to honor these fallen and departed heroes for their bravery, their sacrifice, and their humanity. I ask and pray that we the living, might carry on that legacy."

Few words were spoken as we slowly climbed back into our two tour buses and proceeded through the gate of Arlington National Cemetery. While driving along the muddy sacred streets, the driver of the bus pointed out grave sites of famous Americans buried there: From the Civil War and up to the present, recent graves of veterans from the Gulf War; President John and Jacqueline Kennedy, Ted Kennedy, Senators, Congressmen, Authors, WWII cartoonist Bill Malden, General George Patton; musicians, including Glenn Miller; Joe Lewis; Astronauts, Peter Conrad Jr, Gus Grissom, and Francis Gary Powers, but on that day our group was there for the most significant and meaningful purpose of paying our respects and honoring Company C officer Bill and his wife Edna Pyne.

The cool, damp day continued as we gathered around the wreath brought with us from the 101st Memorial and placed beside the spot where the Pyne couple were laid to rest. Al Hassenzahl stepped on the other side of the headstone, removed his hat and placed it over his

Lest We Forget

heart as he drew us together. "Hello Bill, about eight of us from the old bunch have come by to see you. We just wanted to pay our respects. We missed you at the reunion this year, but we came back together in D.C. to see the new WWII Memorial and the 101st Airborne Memorial before coming over to see you. Well, that's about all, Bill. Oh, except I almost forgot to tell you who's here." Al proceeded with bowed head, as the last remaining commander of Company C to have roll call, and pay his respect with the other seven men standing at attention, saluting, and answering, "Here, Sir."

The eight men of Charlie company, September 30, 2006, salute in honor of their officer Bill Pyne, buried at the Arlington National Cemetery. Shown standing, foreground, Captain Al Hassenzahl; Company C clerk, Norman Smith in wheel chair; and F. Russell Snell in dark jacket and white pants.

Faith, Family, and Future Generations

F. Russell Snell shown standing in front of flak anti-aircraft, anti-tank gun on display at the Palm Springs WWII Air Museum, a reminder of the 88mm Russ saw when the German officer was killed in Normandy, like one that blew him off of the Army Harley motorcycle in Holland, and the one that blew him out of a foxhole in Bastogne, Battle of the Bulge. This particular 88mm was used by German defense in France.

The first reunion of Company C was in Columbus, Ohio, 1976, 31 years after the end of the war and almost 31 years later, we had the last and final reunion for the group. It started with eight men, grew up to over 25 Company C paratroopers and a large fan club. During the reunion years the extended family members and supporters had grown to well over a hundred people, but it had

Lest We Forget

dwindled back down to eight paratroopers from their original Band of Brothers.

On the final night of each annual Company C reunion the veterans met alone without any of the wives or caregivers participating. It was the sole decision of the airborne attending to discuss and vote on the location for the coming year reunion. The year 2006 was different because the men walked away to their undisclosed location carrying canes, pushing walkers, portable oxygen, and being pushed in a wheel chair. The rest of their family and friends were told not to wait up because it might take longer this time. Knowing that this was probably going to be it, the last and final reunion, the men needed a little extra time to say their good-byes. The rest of us could tell by what we saw that the men were emotional and there was a sense of sadness among them.

"I'll just wait in the lobby," I said to Russ. He whispered where they would be, "in the lounge four floors up on the main elevator." I went and sat in the beautiful lobby where I could read and watch for the long meeting to be over when Russ would step through the elevator doors.

The reunion of 1979, coincidentally was also held in Arlington, Virginia when the custom originated to present the group with the "Last Man Standing Bottle of Booze." Since then, each year the well-designed glass bottle was brought to the reunion. It was almost a ritual at the beginning of

Faith, Family, and Future Generations

the weekend, for the work of art to be carefully unpacked, unwrapped, and presented in it's place of prominence for everyone in the group attending to see.

The glass was designed almost true to life in size and color to the real things. It was an artistic replica of a paratrooper's helmet sitting on top of the glass pair of boots. Each year when the names were read of those who had passed away during the previous year, that bottle had more significance and importance. Who would still be standing the coming year? Hopefully they would all return.

Finally Russ stepped off the elevator, turned, and walked towards me, carrying a simple clear disposable plastic cup in his right hand. That was not at all significant to me because he always said, "I like my cold drinks with ice, and my hot drinks, steaming."

"We voted that this was the end of our reunions. Too many of us just aren't able to travel anymore. Five more of our group passed away just this year." Russ paused as he often did while gathering his thoughts when he has something important or emotional to say. "I brought you something."

Russ teared up emotionally and it was then that I realized he was not carrying ice water. There was something very dark in the bottom of the cup. Russ continued, choking up a bit, "This is very special. You're the only lady, in fact you're the only

Lest We Forget

other person, beside the eight of us men, who will have a drink from the 'Last Man Standing Bottle of Liquor.'"

We stood together right in the middle of the busy hallway, while people walked past and around us saying, "Excuse me," but we didn't care. I might not have felt like a lady if I was the only woman drinking with eight men, but alone with Russ while drinking my swallow of aged 27-year-old hard liquor from their canteen, I felt like the luckiest lady in all the world, married to the most thoughtful, sentimental man in Company C.

Because it was their last reunion, the men decided to open the bottle and toast the drink among themselves rather than pass the bottle on to the last living man. The eight were standing together and no one man would have to drink it alone. Without knowing it, the eight men from Charlie Company who shared their "Last Man Standing" drink with a woman, were Al Hassenzahl, James Cadden, Gerald Evers, Ken Parker, Joe Reed, Norm Smith, George Williams and my thoughtful husband, Russ Snell.

I think of Russ gesture to bring me that swallow from their canteen as being like the moment he cut out a piece of his silk parachute from his jump on D-Day. That drink, that moment, he packed my chute.

Not one of the paratroopers would have been upset if they knew what Russ had done. They

Faith, Family, and Future Generations

probably would have wished it was their idea to secretly share a swallow with their wife or caretaker. Russ did it for me and I'm sure if anyone would have questioned or criticized him, Russ would have said, "Blow it out your puckered vent," and they would have all laughed!

"It wouldn't hurt every young man in America to go into the service for a while. It certainly made me grow up in a hurry and take responsibility for my life. The war ended up being much longer than I expected and much tougher than I expected, but I'm a better person for it and that's what gave me such deep appreciation for life," Russ commented.

Facing death can bring out the best in people. We don't decide how or when we're going to die, but we do decide how to live. Russ lived his life with love, compassion, courage and a humble, quiet strength, but he never wanted to talk about himself as if he was anyone special. He felt like he was just one of many. He believed in Currahee, standing alone, but working together. The war makes men who they are. All of his Band of Brothers were special enough that their lives are an example of how to live in the present. The war was what made them the Greatest Generation.

I encouraged Russ to talk about his service and experiences as a paratrooper because his story was important for future generations to learn about. Sharing the pain of life that had a purpose is

Lest We Forget

what inspires and supports others who have difficult decisions to make in their future. When students had the opportunity to meet Russ, it was the reality of actually seeing and talking to a person that they may have just studied about in general. Meeting Russ, gave students a chance to change the hero image from Rock Stars or highly paid athletes to admire someone who actually did something brave and courageous.

Russ was privileged to accept the invitations by our granddaughters, Natalie and Jessica Tomlin to be interviewed by students in the annual Veterans Remembrance Day at Martin Luther King High School, Riverside, California. The Junior History class students and teachers coordinate contributions from the community to provide breakfast and lunch for over 1000 veterans each year. The students Oral History Project has preserved veterans stories for over 15 years and the school has received awards for Best Documentary Short entry into the Academy Awards and their filming has been shown at International Film Festivals across the country and in some foreign countries as well.

Our great-grandson Riley Gunter included Russ to participate with one other WWII veteran who was related to one of the students. Together, veterans from all wars following WWII entered, stood at attention, and answered "Here," when their name was called. Following bugle taps, the roll call

Faith, Family, and Future Generations

honored three of the El Dorado High School, Placentia, California fallen veterans at the memorial built in their honor who were not there to answer when their names were called. The ceremony was a very touching and emotional program, designed by Andrew Binnings, 16 year old Eagle Scout. It gave us incredible pride to see students in both high schools express their appreciation for our servicemen.

The Palm Springs WWII Air Museum archives group, The Desert Sun, radio and television interviewers, Memorial and Veterans Day events have all given Russ an opportunity to speak about memories he had always found it impossible to talk about. Russ was beginning to know what to expect, but it never got easier. He accepted the invitations to educate and tell students that someday they may be asked to sacrifice their life for a friend or for their country. Russ said, "Freedom is not free. It is worth living for, fighting for, and unfortunately sometimes dying for."

Russ admitted to audiences, "I was afraid to talk about the war for so many years because I felt it would bring back too many painful memories and I didn't want anyone to think I wanted sympathy. After the war, my family wanted life to go back to normal and they probably would not have been able to believe the war was as bad as it was. Everyone should be talking about the heroes who died, their grieving families, and not about me. I'm no hero."

Lest We Forget

One day I said, "Russ, you seem more nervous about your interview today than usual. You always do well when you speak and are asked questions. Just keep it simple and if you don't remember something or don't know the answer, just say so. That's alright. You'll be fine."

Russ shook his head and said, "I just wish I had not agreed to this."

"Is there a particular reason this time?"

"No. It's the same reasons every time. I'm afraid I'll be asked how many I killed. I won't answer that." Russ was almost in tears because he has such value for life.

We were talking to Rob and he said emphatically, with understanding and support, "No one should ever ask that. I don't blame you, Russ. You don't need to ever answer that."

Russ responded appreciatively, "Thanks. I just wish I knew how many lives I saved. How many lived because America and our Allies sacrificed so much with the blood of so many of our best young men."

Rick said it so well when he called one Veterans Day to thank Russ for his service, "Your bravery to volunteer your service, knowing when you entered the war that you would probably die, is real courage."

It brought tears to my eyes, as I thought how difficult it has been on Russ's entire life to have that on his mind: knowing that at any moment during

Faith, Family, and Future Generations

the war he might die and to know he shot and killed a person. Seeing and facing death has a way of changing a person, never to be the same again. Russ's family wanted life to be normal again, but after fighting in a war there was no normal. Lest we forget, every family member has the opportunity to remember and tell others about the painful sacrifice of each one of our servicemen. The paratroopers did it for us. They packed our parachute to give us a safe landing.

On the 70th Anniversary, August 14, 2015, celebrating and honoring the end of WWII, Russ was presented with three tributes at a Spirit of '45 program, Palm Desert, California. The event was coordinated by Dr. Dave Thompson from the Palm Springs WWII Air Museum:

California State 28th District Senator Jeff Stone presented a Certificate of Recognition expressing appreciation because the lives of "our Greatest Generation will ensure that their example of courage, shared sacrifice, can do attitude, service to others and the national unity will continue to inspire future generations- especially our youth."

"Your honorable and heroic service will forever inspire current and future generations of Americans to come together to work for the continued betterment of the United States and the World," was beautifully printed on the framed plaque from John U. Benoit, Riverside County, Fourth District Supervisor. A gold border around

Lest We Forget

the Certificate of Congressional Recognition from Doctor Raul Ruiz, House of Representatives, expressed "gratitude for your valiant service and your legacy as a guardian of freedom."

A couple of weeks later, the door bell rang and I was given a special delivery package for Russ from the Embassy of Belgium in Washington D.C. Enclosed was the Citation for the Belgian Fourragere 70th Anniversary Celebration, ending the Battle of the Bulge and stated, "you participated in the largest land battle ever fought by the United States Army and contributed to a monumental victory over the enemy that also laid the foundation of lasting peace in Europe. Belgium will never forget your achievement." It was accompanied with the beautiful braided burgundy Fourragere, mounted in a black shadow box frame.

Whenever Russ received an award, certificate, or recognition, he felt humbly that he was accepting it on behalf of the sacrifices of many. Whenever he was honored or publicly acknowledged, Russ believed it belonged to those who were unable to be there or were killed in action. He accepted for those who could not do the same. Russ's hope is that by witnessing a public presentation to him it is lest we forget the sacrifices of all our servicemen and his Band of Brothers. The awards and medals that Russ received from WWII are the Bronze Star, Purple Heart and two bronze Oak Leaf Clusters, Good Conduct Medal, Presi-

Faith, Family, and Future Generations

dential Unit Citation, European-African Middle Eastern Campaign Medal, World War II Victory Medal, Combat Infantryman Badge First Award, Honorable Service Lapel WWII Button, Marksman Badge, Rifle Badge; the "Chevalier" (Knight) of the Legion of Honor from France, the Orange Lanyard from the Netherlands; Belgium's Croix de Guerre and Fourragere.

Allied and American survivors of the war lived with the hope and will to find peace that seemed impossible amidst the chaos of the war. Having their own sons being drafted or already in the war, seeing loved ones killed, and hearing of destroyed homes and devastated people, affected the servicemen and family members. During battle, the 101st fell back on their training and believed in themselves. They looked at the big picture and the future with confidence that they had no choice but to go on, think positive, and survive.

When the war was over, coming home was bittersweet. The celebration and joyous victory should never be forgotten and Americans are given that opportunity every year at patriotic ceremonies, holidays, and parades. Russ was glad when the world quit spinning so that he could get off of the carousel parade in his post traumatic mind. He celebrated being "Home Alive in '45," but he would never forget the injustice of the unfathomable war he had witnessed and suffered.

Lest We Forget

Russ's story was not about forgiveness nor revenge. It was about the pain of war, death, the good and evil of man, but it was primarily about the future. To honor all who serve, all who sacrificed their life, and all who protect our country are values worth expressing gratitude for. Americans must continue to appreciate our freedom, independence, and that all men are created equal. Russ fought for the values of his country, the constitution, and all freedom-loving people to have their God given right to worship, freedom of the press, speech, right to assemble, and have a fair trial.

We were rushing down the hall of the Los Angeles airport to make connections for our vacation to Hawaii in 2012. A stewardess and pilot noticed Russ's struggle pulling the larger bag. The attendant said, "Let us help you with that," and they also got Russ a wheel chair. When the gates opened to the plane, Russ's wheel chair was driven across the ramp, right up the airplane aisle, and he was seated first.

The stewardess at the door welcomed us and I waited with her until they could bring the wheel chair back down the aisle. While Russ was being seated, I commented to the hostess, "My husband loves to fly. He says it's a lot better than jumping out of planes anymore!"

"Military?"

"Yes. He was a 101st Airborne paratrooper."

"Where?" She asked with interest.

Faith, Family, and Future Generations

"He jumped in Normandy, Holland, and fought in the Battle of the Bulge," I replied.

She was taking a mental note because once in flight the speaker came on and the pilot introduced himself and then announced, "It is a pleasure for me to welcome each passenger, but one in particular. We are privileged to have with us today a guest I would like to honor. Mr. Russell Snell, 101st Airborne paratrooper, who jumped on D-Day in the Normandy Invasion. He parachuted again into Holland, and went by truck to the Battle of the Bulge, in Bastogne. Mr. Snell would you please raise your hand so that we can see where you are seated?"

The entire crew and passengers aboard the crowded plane broke into loud applause as Russ humbly raised his hand and looked at me in complete surprise for the unexpected recognition. It was a gift for us to experience the patriotism of the passengers as they shook Russ's hand. During the five hour flight, passengers went out of their way to thank Russ and said, "You're an American hero. Our country is forever grateful. What a privilege to meet you. God bless you, Sir."

When we landed, a stewardess offered Russ a wheel chair, but after resting during flight, he smiled appreciatively, "No, I'll be just fine getting off. Thank you very much." Again, Russ was honored by letting us off the plane first. As we walked down the ramp, both pilots and crew were standing at the

Lest We Forget

end of the ladder, waiting to salute and shake Russ's hand.

Russ complemented them right back, "Thank you. Good job. Nice flight." Lest we forget to thank our servicemen, that was a flight that I doubt any passenger or crew would ever forget and neither would we.

EPILOGUE

To live through a war after three injuries, creates a great appreciation for life and so Russell and Marjorie Snell celebrate every June 6 anniversary of D-Day more than his own birthday.

Perhaps Russ's most common of many expressions, is "I love you yet today," and that led to the discussion that Russ and Marjorie decided to not just express their love but to say why they love each other. On his D-Day birthday one year, Marjorie wrote to him:

"Russ, you know that poem by Elizabeth Barrett Browning, "Why do I love you...let me count the ways!" Well, because you are my favorite 101st airborne paratrooper hero, I have written 101 words describing you alphabetically, 101 reasons why I love you:

A – Airborne're Able, Accomplished, Accurate, Aggressive, Awesome
B – Bold, Brave, Bounce
C – Camaraderie, Courageous, Conviction, Capable, Compelling, Clever
D – Dedicated, Determined, Dependable, Defenders
E – Efficient, Energetic, Endurance, Encouraging
F – Focused, Fast, Fearless, Faithful
G – Guided, Goal-oriented
H – Healthy, Honorable, Hard-working, Honest, Heroic, Hopeful, Handsome

Lest We Forget

I – Idolized, Involved
J – Jumper, Just
K – Knowledgeable, Keen
L – Love of and Loyal to God and Country, Legendary, Liberators, Logical
M – Magnificent, Manly
N – Notorious
O – Optimistic, Organized, Original
P – Patriotic, Practiced, Practical, Prepared, Professional, Polished, Prompt, Pioneer, Powerful, Paratrooper
Q – Qualified, Quality
R – Respectful, Resolved, Resourceful, Rigorous, Restorer of Dignity, Rendezvous with destiny
S – Strong, Smart, Sincere, Spiritual, Skillful, Sharp-shooter, Soldier, Spirited, Sacrificial, Selfless
T – Trained, Triumphant, Thoughtful, Thankful, Trustworthy
U – Unwavering
V – Victorious, Virtuous, Valued, Volunteer
W – Winner, Wise, Willing
X – eXcels, eXtremely proud of America
Y – Youthful, Young-at-heart, Yearns for freedom
Z – Zealous, Zon liberators

About the Author: Marjorie A. Snell, registered nurse graduate from Loma Linda University and Riverside City College, taught many student nurses during their specialty rotation. During her 20 years of experience in surgical, cardiac, neurology, and pediatric intensive care units, she acquired the skills to be on the Policy and Procedure Committee for eight years, reviewing and writing for the Riverside County Hospital Procedure Manual. Marjorie compiled and wrote the Pediatric Intensive Care Manual, 1984. For five years Mrs. Snell was Office Manager and Supervisor of the Riverside County Hospital Eye Clinic. These experiences led her to being elected as a member of the Building Committee for the County Hospital in Moreno Valley. She was the Riverside County Nurses Association Chapter secretary for three years before moving to the Coachella Valley. During the past twenty years during retirement, she developed her artistic and writing skills by taking classes and becoming President of the Spa City Paletteers Art Club for seven years. With the Historical Society archive group, she co-authored the book for the Arcadia Publishers publication, Desert Hot Springs.

ACKNOWLEDGMENTS AND CREDITS: Once my husband Francis Russell Snell was comfortable enough to talk about WWII, our family and friends became the inspiration to write and preserve his paratrooper stories they love to hear. Russ's daughters Jane Wood, Lisa Hindsley; Marjorie's children Robert and Richard Tomlin, Tanya Turley; our family and grandchildren contributed by knowing what to ask and how to say it. I am especially appreciative of Christopher Eastman, Natalie Tomlin, and Brittany Turley for their work in editing and proofreading.

The treasure trove of fascinating details were acquired from Russ's Currahee 506 album, 1945, our reunion visits with his fellow 101st Airborne paratroopers, and 31 years of 506, Company C scrapbooks. Major Franklin Foster was known as "picture taker" and is believed to have taken the Snell photographs shown in the Currahee album. Other photographers for Charlie company were Jules Chicoine and Pat Irving Fitzig.

The talks by Norman Smith, Company C, and Lieutenant Colonel Jan Kenneth Gleiman, were valuable contributions that confirm our value and appreciation for Russ's Band of Brothers. Without the paratroopers this book would not have been possible.

I wish to thank Dr. David Thompson, Veterans History Project and the late Ralph Medcalf, Assistant Librarian and docent of the Palm Springs

Lest We Forget

WWII Air Museum for their assistance and encouragement, with special thanks to Robert Andrade, Historian and Librarian, who earned my immeasurable gratitude for his unlimited knowledge of history, research, advice, and editing assistance.

I am most grateful for the contribution of James Bishop, Author, for providing guidance, editing, text format, digitizing of photography, and coordinating the project with the publishers.

This book was written as accurate and true to history as possible without claiming to be historians, because it is told by two people who fell in love almost 45 years after the war. It was written from our family stories, photographs and emotional memories, but for my husband, Francis Russell Snell, I am forever grateful for telling me your story, for your love, devotion, patriotism and sacrifice for America.

CPSIA information can be obtained at www.ICGtesting.com
Printed in the USA
BVOW08s2159130716
455513BV00001B/48/P